KU-615-066

CHARMING
SMALL HOTEL
GUIDES

France

Bed &
Breakfast

CHARMING SMALL HOTEL GUIDES

France

Bed & Breakfast

Edited by Paul Wade & Kathy Arnold

DUNCAN PETERSEN

HUNTER
PUBLISHING INC

300 Raritan Center Parkway,
CN 94, Edison, N.J. 08818

Copyright © Paul Wade, Kathy Arnold 1995
© Duncan Petersen Publishing Ltd 1995

All rights reserved. No reproduction, copy or transmission of this
publication may be made without written permission. No
paragraph of this publication may be reproduced, copied or
transmitted save with written permission or in accordance with
the provisions of the Copyright Act 1956 (as amended). Any
person who does any unauthorized act in relation to this
publication may be liable to criminal prosecution and civil claims
for damages.

Conceived, designed and produced by
Duncan Petersen Publishing Ltd,
Edited by Team Wade

Editors	Paul Wade, Kathy Arnold
Principal inspectors	Lucy Blogg, Sue and James Bartholomew
Additional inspectors	Nick Arbin, Sarah Bew, James Brown, Steve Caspar, Roger Ford, Michelle Hall, Louis James, Kim Fortuny, John Mabbett, Nicola Swallow, Sharon Thomas
Art director	Mel Petersen

This edition published in the UK and Commonwealth 1995 by
Duncan Petersen Publishing Ltd,
31 Ceylon Road, London W14 OYP.

Sales representation in the UK and Ireland by
World Leisure Marketing,
117 The Hollow, Littleover, Derby DE3 7BS.

Distributed by
Grantham Book Services

ISBN 1 872576 51 6

A CIP catalogue record for this book is available
from the British Library

AND

Published in the USA 1995 by
Hunter Publishing Inc.,
300 Raritan Center Parkway, CN 94, Edison, N.J. 08818.
Tel (908) 225 1900 Fax (908) 417 0482

ISBN 1-55650-677-5

Typeset by Duncan Petersen Publishing Ltd
Originated by Reprocolor International S.R.I., Milan
Printed by G. Canale & Co SpA, Turin

Contents

Introduction

With this, the ninth book in the *Charming Small Hotel Guides* series, we take a timely and interesting departure: an expert and in-depth assessment of the growing number of bed-and-breakfasts in France.

A few years ago, bed-and-breakfast (*chambre d'hôtes*) was a novelty for the French, often limited to the north-west of the country where farmers welcomed British visitors who were used to the idea of paying to stay in a private home. Now *chambre d'hôtes* signs are to be seen the length and breadth of the country: in hedgerows and among mountain pine trees; nailed to humble gateposts; attached to grandiose château gates.

Although they offer a bedroom, breakfast and, perhaps, an evening meal, these are not small hotels, nor are the owners professional hoteliers. Nevertheless, good bed-and-breakfasts in France are as true to the *Charming Small Hotel Guide* philosophy as any small hotel. Their rooms look like real bedrooms; meals are carefully prepared, using local produce and following regional recipes; hosts take a genuine interest in their guests. Above all, the atmosphere is personal, the experience special. They even offer a sense of adventure for travellers who, by staying in a bed-and-breakfast, will discover corners of France that they would otherwise never find.

Chambres d'hôtes come in all shapes and sizes: from imposing châteaux with aristocratic owners to working farms where the smell of the countryside hits you full in the nostrils. There are converted *bastides* (fortified farmhouses) in southern France, wooden chalets in the mountains, watermills by streams and fishermens' cottages. Many are in or around France's most popular tourist regions. As yet, only a handful are in cities.

For foreign visitors, staying in a *chambre d'hôtes* is an opportunity to meet the locals and experience the French way of life. The French are also taking to this new way of travelling in their own country, rediscovering their roots. They used to stay in one and two star hotels but, sadly, these no longer offer such attractive value for money. Even the 'good little local restaurant' is harder to find.

For all these reasons, we believe that France's *chambres d'hôtes* are more than just an alternative for the holiday-maker and even those travelling on business. There has never been a better time to try bed-and-breakfast, French-style.

The inspectors
Our selection has been made after thorough research, personal recommendations and expert assessment by a small, trained team of inspectors chosen by the editors.
No *chambre d'hôtes* pays to be in this guide.

Introduction

Selection process

The boom in bed-and-breakfasts in France has tempted many families to open their doors to visitors. Some offer no more than a *chambre d'amis* (a spare room); others are unused to welcoming strangers into their homes. Our inspectors, alert to these considerations, drove thousands of kilometers all over France, searching for the best at every price level. They prodded mattresses, checked the bathrooms, listened for traffic noise, tasted local dishes and, most important of all, talked to hosts in order to discover whether they possessed the human touch essential for running a pleasant *chambre d'hôtes*. Scores failed these tests.

In the end, we found more than 400 which met our standards. Of each we can honestly say that we would be happy to spend the night there. That, however, does not mean that they are all faultless. Just as there is praise in our descriptions, so there is criticism.

Everyone has his or her own idea of the perfect bed-and-breakfast. Not everyone enjoys the smells of a working farm; on the other hand, parents of small children would not be comfortable in a house filled with priceless antiques.

We believe it is important to 'tell it like it is', so that readers can decide what will suit them best, for an overnight stop, a weekend break or a holiday by the sea. So, we spell out what is on offer: whether bedrooms are in the owners' house or in a separate building; whether the *table d'hôtes* (an evening meal) is value for money; whether children are welcome and pets accepted. If you read a note of criticism in a description, it does not mean a bed-and-breakfast is not worth considering.

Size

In the main, our selections have between three and seven bedrooms, but some offer only one, while a few have a dozen. In many *chambres d'hôtes* in the countryside, outbuildings have been converted into guest accommodation, offering more privacy.

Facilities

A surprising number have a swimming-pool and tennis court, though saunas are rare. Since these are family homes, there are often bicycles and table-tennis for children (and adults) to use. There may be a sitting-room where guests relax or perhaps a kitchen for preparing simple meals or picnics. This is obviously a boon for families.

Bedrooms

Rooms vary in size and furnishings. Some have four-poster

beds, others are suited to families, with extra beds for children. Our inspectors were impressed by the quality, particularly when compared with old-fashioned hotels.

Bathrooms
One of our inspectors is a self-confessed fanatic about cleanliness, especially when it comes to bathrooms and WCs. She has been known to travel with her own bottle of bleach, but even she had to admit that the standards of hygiene in *chambres d'hôtes* were high. "With only a few exceptions, they were spotlessly clean," she reported. Although the more luxurious homes may have toiletries in the bathrooms, some simple places do not, so it is advisable to take your own soap and shampoo.

With a few exceptions, the selections in this guide have a private bathroom and WC for each guest bedroom.

Gîtes de France
Many of the bed-and-breakfasts listed are registered with the French national organisation, Gîtes de France. Expect to see their green, yellow and red logo identifying a *chambre d'hôtes*.

Nowadays, there are thousands of establishments, rated for their facilities. We go further, assessing the personality of the hosts and their welcome, the beauty of the location and the quality of the evening meal.

Table d'hôtes
In a country famous for its cuisine, it is perhaps not surprising that eating is an important part of the *chambre d'hôtes* experience. Unlike the British tradition of bed-and-breakfast, many French hosts provide an evening meal. This is a chance to sample authentic local dishes, using local produce and accompanied by, of course, local wines, ciders or beers. This may be served at separate tables, or guests may gather at one large table. Inevitably, any language barriers are overcome as conversation begins with 'where do you come from?' and progresses to discussions of sport, national customs and politics.

Châteaux
Staying in the stately homes of France has been an option for many years. The best offer a chance to experience 'how the other half lives', with luxurious accommodation, memorable meals and attentive hosts. Unfortunately, there are some owners, however, who seem to think guests should be grateful to stay in their châteaux, even if the plumbing is antiquated and the welcome off hand.

Introduction

Credit cards
Credit cards are not universally accepted by bed-and-breakfasts. Eurocheques and travellers' cheques are usually welcome but it is always advisable to double-check when booking.

Stopovers and holidays
Chambres d'hôtes in France fill many needs. For some visitors, they are just an overnight stop; for others, they are places to spend a whole holiday. Remember that the longer the stay, the greater the reduction in price. On the other hand, some owners insist on a minimum stay in high season.

Look for a base in a tourist area such as Provence, the Loire Valley or Normandy. Consider a bed-and-breakfast if you are skiing in the Alps or visiting Paris. Staying with a family means that you learn more about the region than other tourists do, thanks to local tips on shopping, eating and sight-seeing.

Ferry services
When it comes to crossing the English Channel, British visitors to France have more route options with Stena Sealink Line: Dover to Calais, Newhaven to Dieppe and Southampton to Cherbourg. Each port has swift access to France's motorway network.

Dover to Calais: journey time $1^1\!2$ hours, 25 sailings a day in each direction
Newhaven to Dieppe: journey time 4 hours, 4 sailings a day in each direction
Southampton to Cherbourg: journey time $4^1\!2$ hours (daytime) or overnight, up to 2 sailings a day in each direction

Reservations: Stena Sealink Line
Charter House
Park Street
Ashford
Kent TN24 8EX
Tel: (01233) 647047

Electricity
Do not expect *chambres d'hôtes* to have international sockets. Be sure to take whatever adaptor is necessary for your electric razor or hairdrier.

The do's and don'ts of *chambre d'hôtes*
Staying in a hotel is straightforward but a bed-and-breakfast is, after all, someone's home. How should you behave? We asked the young owner of one small château to give a

guide to the etiquette of staying in a *chambre d'hôtes*.

Do ...
... remember that a *chambre d'hôtes* is still a home; respect our privacy as we respect yours.
... telephone to book your room, the earlier the better;
...telephone if you get lost, expect to arrive later than planned ... or if you have to cancel the reservation.
... go to bed (and get up) at a reasonable hour. The hosts who cleaned up after dinner will have to get up to prepare breakfast as well.
... talk to hosts about the area. We are all proud of our regions, the customs, attractions and special foods.
... ask if your hosts mind smoking. Many old houses are now non-smoking.
... inform your hosts of any dietary or mobility problems you may have **when you book**.

Don't...
... expect anyone to carry your luggage to your room. Hosts may offer to help but we are not hotel porters.
... expect anyone to babysit for your children ... or your pets.
... expect an evening meal to be provided automatically; hosts may offer *table d'hôtes* but usually at a set time. We are not running restaurants.
... expect to make your own bed. Usually that is done for guests.
... expect to tip anyone.

Having said all that, treat us as you would want to be treated by visitors in your own home.

These do's and don'ts are the views of Charles-Henry de Valbray, who lives in the **Château de St-Paterne,** near Alençon. He is one of many owners who have decided to welcome guests into their mansions. Rooms are filled with antiques, paintings and large mirrors. Bedrooms are atmospheric, with painted ceilings, tall windows and creaking boards. An evening meal is an occasion, with silver candelabra, wine in decanters and elegant china. The ambience is that of a dinner party in the home of a friend. It all adds up to an experience which can be the highlight of a holiday.

Both sides benefit. "For guests, it is a chance to learn about and experience another side of French life," says Charles-Henry. "For the owners, it is also important. Our guests are enabling us to preserve our *patrimoine,* our heritage. " He happens to live in a château but his rules apply even to the humblest farmhouse.

Introduction

How this guide is organized

Overall, entries are arranged geographically. France is divided into 9 regions. Within each region, entries are organized alphabetically by the initial letter of the village, town or entry with which they are most readily linked.

First, North-western France which includes Brittany and Normandy; then we move through the Ile-de-France which surrounds Paris, and on to North-eastern France which follows the Belgian border from the coast to Alsace-Lorraine and the border with Germany.

Next, Western France which embraces the Loire valley with its famous châteaux. Then we continue to Eastern France with its great wine-growing areas of Burgundy plus the grandeur of the Alps on the Swiss border.

South-western France also boasts well-known vineyards around Bordeaux and includes the Pyrenees and the Basque country bordering Spain. Inland is the Dordogne.

Central France is essentially the Massif Central; it is one of the country's least-known and least populated areas, with a rugged landscape and remote villages. Bed-and-breakfasts here cater for those who enjoy the great outdoors.

The South of France is known for its luxury hotels and apartment blocks. Even here, however, the *chambre d'hôtes* movement is growing.

By contrast, there are only a few bed-and-breakfasts in Corsica. Here the accommodation may be simpler than elsewhere in France but the welcome is just as warm.

Maps

Each area has its own map, with the locations of bed-and-breakfasts marked and page references (p16-31).

Entries

The major entries are in the front of the book, two to a page, many with a colour photograph. These are our warmest recommendations.

At the back of the book are shorter entries, four to a page. These are by no means 'second-class' *chambres d'hôtes*. Some may have only one or two rooms, others are heavily booked, still others are difficult to get to. For reasons such as these, we feel they do not justify a half-page. Nevertheless, we are enthusiastic about **all** of them.

How to find an entry

There are three easy ways to find a bed-and-breakfast:

Use the maps between pages 16-31. The numbers on the map refer to the page in the guide where the bed-and-breakfast is featured.

If you know the area you want to visit, browse through that section until you find a place that fits the bill.

Introduction

Use the index at the back which lists entries by their location (p199-207).

How to read an entry

At the top of the page is the area of France. Below that is the town or village with a directional 'locator' eg W of Tours (west of Tours) as an orientation point on the map. For this, we strongly advise using a large scale road atlas. Finally, the name of the house itself or, in some cases where there is no name, the hamlet or street address.

Fact boxes

Beneath each *chambre d'hôtes* description are the facts and figures which should help you to decide whether or not it is within your price range and has the facilities you require.

Tel

French telephone numbers have eight digits and have no extra codes when calling within the country. The exception is the Paris region, which has a '1' at the beginning. When telephoning within this area, you do not need to use the '1'. When phoning the capital from the provinces, or vice versa, preface the entire number with 16.

Fax

Many *chambres d'hôtes* have a fax number so it is easy to confirm a telephone booking.

Prices

The range of prices are for a room for two, with breakfast. There is no high or low season, so rates are the same year-round.

F ....up to 150 FF
FF ....150 - 300 FF
FFF ....300 - 450 FF
FFFF ....over 450 FF

Evening meal

Some hosts do not offer dinner, since there are often places to eat nearby. 'By request only' indicates those who do, but guests must give their hosts advance warning. The evening meal, or *table d'hôtes*, can vary in price from 70 FF to as much as 300 FF per head. Where meals are particularly well-priced, we say so in the text, as we do when we think they are expensive.

It is important to ask if the price includes aperitifs, wine and coffee. What seems to be a bargain can become expensive if drinks are extra. In general, large portions are the rule. The more expensive *tables d'hôtes*, especially in châteaux, reflect the fine china, crystal and silver which make these meals special.

Introduction

Credit cards
We use the following abbreviations for credit cards:
AE   American Express
DC   Diners Club
MC   Master Card/Access/Eurocard
V   Visa/Barclaycard/Bank Americard/Carte Bleue

Children
Children are welcome in most hotels and restaurants in France. *Chambres d'hôtes* are no exception; however, some homes are so full of heirlooms that our inspectors suggest parents would not feel comfortable staying here with their children.

Disabled
Most owners are willing to help but few homes are adapted for wheelchairs, especially the bathrooms. Some, however, have bedrooms on the ground floor. Discuss individual needs by telephone beforehand with the owner. Lifts/elevators are virtually non-existent.

Pets
Even when we indicate that pets are welcome, hosts emphasise that they must be well-trained.

Closed
Do double-check the exact dates of closing. Even those hosts who say they never close may decide to take a break in winter.

Languages
Although more and more hosts speak a foreign language, they are delighted when guests speak in French and encourage even those who are not fluent.

Proprietors
Although the majority of hosts are French, there are some British and Dutch owners who offer *chambre d'hôtes* and are just as knowledgeable about their regions as any local.

And finally ...
We cannot stress enough how necessary it is to telephone hosts ahead of time. The best homes are the most popular, even 'out of season'. Moreover, where hotels are usually in towns, many bed-and-breakfasts are deep in the countryside, off the beaten track.

   We have endeavoured to give clear directions but small country roads twist and turn. Signs can be confusing. Many hosts will post or fax maps when rooms are booked. This can save time and frustration.

Introduction

Confirming a booking

It is well worth booking a room in advance for the peak holiday seasons. Nowadays, many *chambres d'hôtes* have a fax which makes confirmation of a telephone reservation easier. The following is a simple letter that can be amended as needed:

Dear Sir, Madam,

I would like to book a room for two from ..... to ..... (dates) for ..... nights. Could you confirm the booking and the price of the room as soon as possible.

Yours faithfully,

....

(name)

Monsieur, Madame,

Je voudrais réserver une chambre pour deux personnes à partir du ..... au ..... pour ..... nuits. Veuillez confirmer la réservation et le prix de la chambre dès que possible.

Nous vous prions d'agréer l'expression de nos sentiments distingués,

....

(name)

Tourist information

For further information about any part of France, contact the French National Tourist Office (Maison de la France).

In the UK: 178 Piccadilly
                    London W1V OAL
                    Tel: 0891 244123
                    Fax: 0171 493 6594

In the USA: 610 Fifth Avenue, Suite 222
                    New York, NY 10020-2452
                    Tel: 212 757 1125
                    Fax: 212 247 6468

                    645 North Michigan Avenue
                    Chicago, IL 60611-2836
                    Tel: 312 337 6301
                    Fax: 312 337 6339

                    9454 Wilshire Boulevard
                    Beverly Hills, CA 90912-2967
                    Tel: 310 271 7838
                    Fax: 310 276 2835

                    2305 Cedar Springs Road
                    Suite 205, Dallas TX 75201
                    Tel: 214 720 4010
                    Fax: 214 720 0250

National and school holidays

It is important to book in advance – first by telephone, followed by a confirming letter or fax – for the peak holiday periods, particularly in the summer. From mid-July to the end of August, not only are the French vacationing at the seaside and in the country, holidaymakers from abroad are also visiting France.

New Year's Day	January 1
Easter	March/April
Labour Day	May 1
Armistice Day	May 8
Ascension Day	May 12
Whitsun	long weekend, late May
Bastille Day	July 14
Assumption Day	mid-August
All Saints' Day	November 1
Remembrance Day	November 11
Christmas Day	December 25

Hotel location maps

Maps of hotel locations

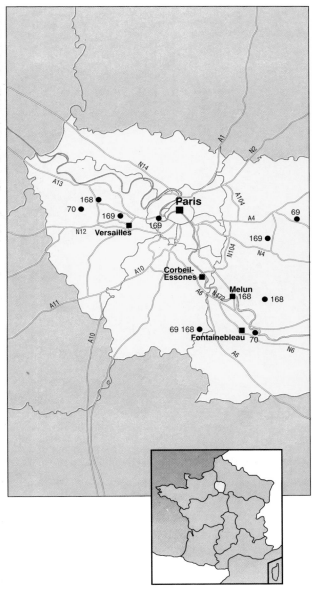

Although many homes in Paris have a *chambre d'amis* (spare room) for bed-and-breakfast, most prefer to work with an agency rather than deal direct with the public. Nevertheless, we do have a list of homes around the capital that make a useful base for visiting both Paris and Euro Disney.

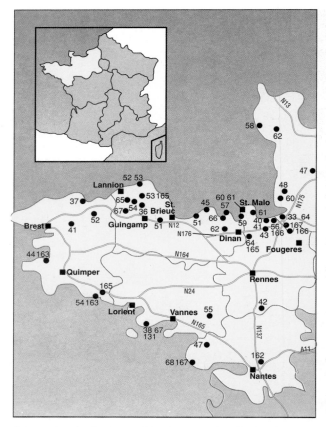

Brittany is a land of rugged landscapes, of rocky shoreline and beaches washed by the waves of the Atlantic. The north coast has pink granite, the western extreme of Finisterre (Land's End) is still untamed, the southern coastline is popular with sailors for its bays and coves while families with small children enjoy the sandy beaches. In the *Armor*, the Breton name for the 'land of the sea', villages can look sombre thanks to granite walls and small windows. There is a simplicity about life here and traditions, such as the Breton language, remain despite the fact that Brittany is France's second most popular summer holiday area, after the Mediterranean.

The *chambre d'hôtes* movement is well-established in Brittany, with places to stay both on the coast and inland but the best are booked up early for the school holidays

North-Western France

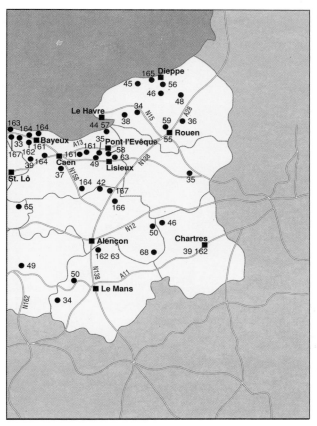

Thanks to its image of apple orchards, cows and half-timbered, thatched cottages, Normandy is one of France's most distinctive regions. Sights such as Le Mont-St-Michel, the Bayeux Tapestry, Rouen Cathedral and the D-Day beaches of the Second World War attract visitors all year round. Within the area is a surprising variety of landscapes. The Cotentin Peninsula has spectacular dark cliffs at the north-western tip but on the coastline between the busy ports of Le Havre and Dieppe, the chiselled cliffs are chalky white. Caen is a bustling city with plenty of history, while the fishing village of Honfleur exemplifies the word 'picturesque'.

Our inspectors appreciated the comfort and easy welcome offered by hosts in Normandy, who are used to having visitors from all over the world.

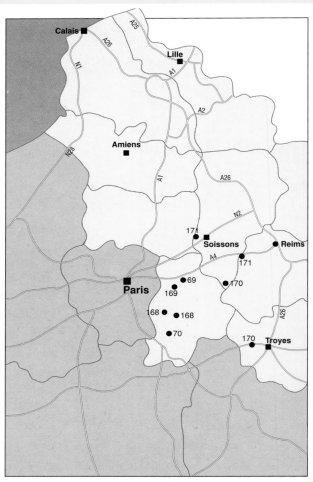

The flat, open fields which stretch inland from Calais to the industrial cities of Lille and the coal fields beyond are little more than a flash in most visitors' rear view mirrors. Battles, usually involving the English, have been fought here for centuries right through to the First World War. Although many may use the bed-and-breakfasts here purely as stopovers, this is an area well worth exploring.

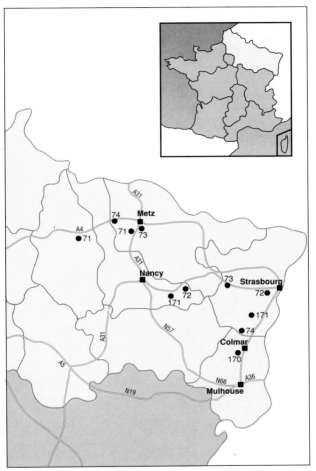

In Alsace-Lorraine, houses in medieval villages look like illustrations for childrens' fairy tales. We think this visual mixture of Germany and France is one of the prettiest regions of France, yet it is less-visited than many other parts of the country. As yet, the *chambres d'hôtes* concept is new here; we hope that, as the idea catches on, more quality places will offer rooms, particularly in the delightful old towns.

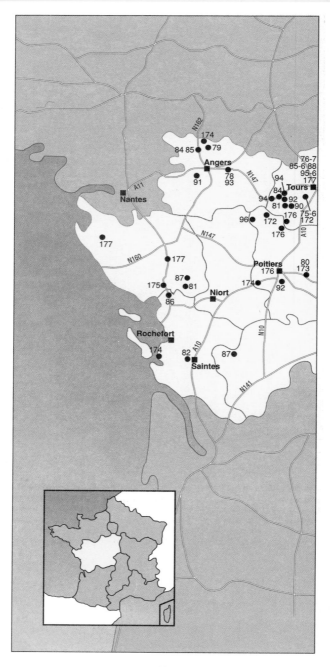

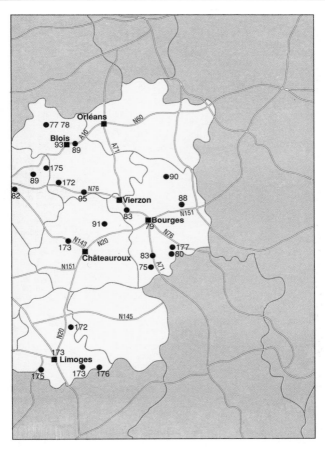

This region wraps itself around one of the world's major tourist 'honey pots': the Loire valley. The châteaux of Chambord and Azay-le-Rideau, Chenonceau and Villandry attract millions of visitors every year. There is much more to see, however, including the towns of Angers and Saumur and the vineyards and villages. You can also get off the beaten track into 'undiscovered' countryside. *Chambre d'hôtes* hosts will be happy to help.

Eastern France

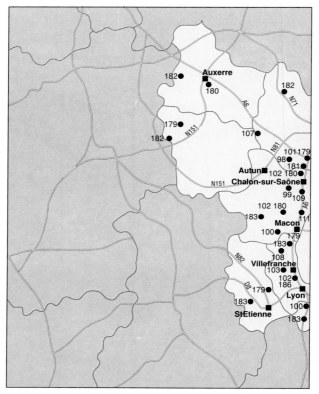

This is an area of contrasts. To the west is Burgundy, with its vineyards and towns made wealthy by some of the world's greatest wines. To the east are the Alpine ski slopes. Our inspectors found bed-and-breakfasts to suit wine-lovers, cyclists, walkers and skiers.

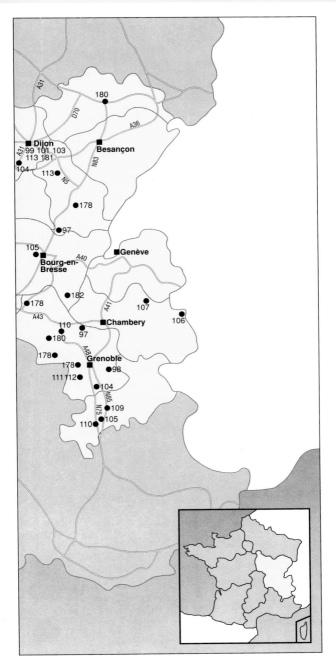

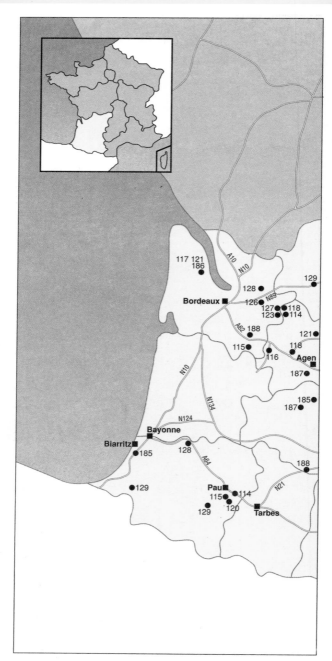

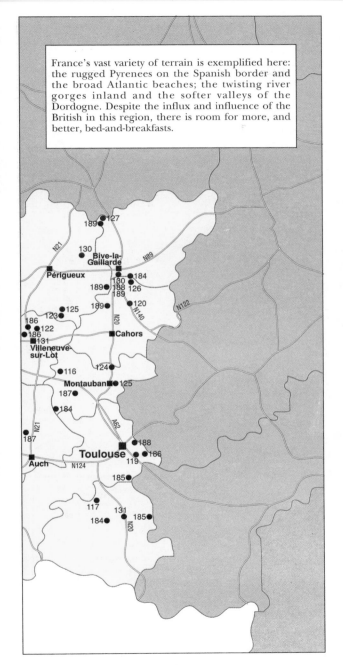

France's vast variety of terrain is exemplified here: the rugged Pyrenees on the Spanish border and the broad Atlantic beaches; the twisting river gorges inland and the softer valleys of the Dordogne. Despite the influx and influence of the British in this region, there is room for more, and better, bed-and-breakfasts.

Central France

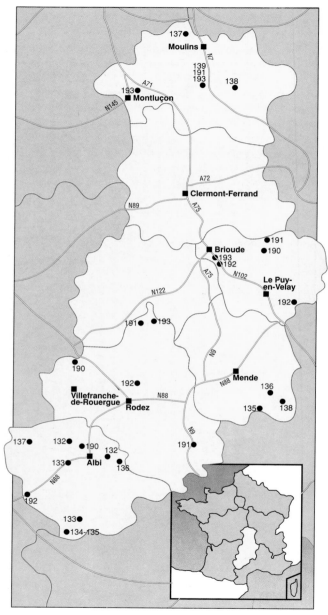

These seven *départements* are rugged, untamed, invigoratingly unspoiled. *Chambres d'hôtes* are few and far between here.

Corsica

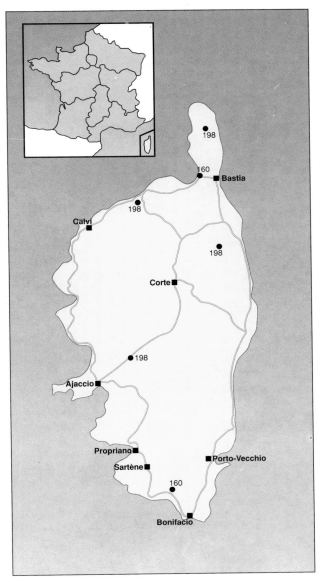

The island divides into two areas: the beaches that are busy in summer and the almost empty mountains which are often a test of drivers' skill. *Chambres d'hôtes* are rare. Standards are not yet high enough to suit sophisticated visitors but there are plain and simple places with welcoming hosts.

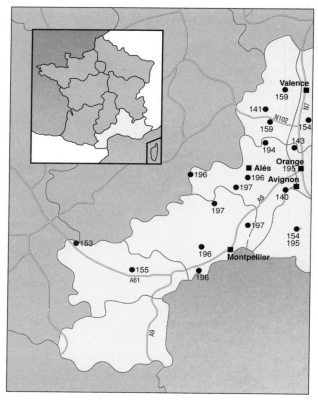

From the glamour of the Côte d'Azur to the modern holiday flats of Languedoc-Roussillon, the South of France is a popular summer playground. Just inland, however, is peace and quiet, even in summer. This is where we found some delightful *chambres d'hôtes*, offering excellent value for money in an area where hotel prices are high. The bed-and-breakfast idea is just taking off here.

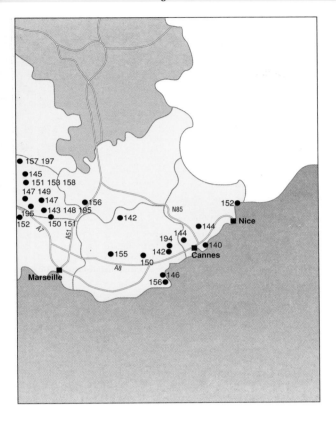

Reporting to the guide

Please write and tell us about your experiences of bed-and-breakfasts, small hotels and inns, whether good or bad, whether listed in this edition or not. As well as bed-and-breakfasts in France, we are interested in charming small hotels in: Britain, Ireland, Italy, France, Spain, Portugal, Germany, Austria, Switzerland and other European countries, as well as the east and west coasts of the United States.

The address to write to is:
The Editors
France Bed-and-Breakfast
Charming Small Hotel Guides
Duncan Petersen Publishing Ltd.
31 Ceylon Road
London W14 0YP
England

Checklist
Please use a separate sheet of paper for each report; include your name, address and telephone number on each report.

Your reports will be received with particular pleasure if they are typed, and if they are organized under the following headings:
   Name of establishment
   Town or village it is in, or nearest
   Full address, including post code
   Telephone number
   Time and duration of visit
   The building and setting
   The public rooms
   The bedrooms and bathrooms
   Physical comfort (chairs, beds, heat, light, hot water)
   Standards of maintenance and housekeeping
   Atmosphere, welcome and service
   Food
   Value for money

We assume that in writing you have no objection to your views being published unpaid, either verbatim or in an edited version. Names of major outside contributors are acknowledged in the guide, at the editors' discretion.

Aignerville, NW of Bayeux

Manoir de l'Hormette

It is hard to believe that this carefully restored 17thC stone house was once a farm. Bedrooms are in three buildings: the main house, across the courtyard and, set apart, La Bretonnière, which we recommend for family holidays. Overall, the look is practical rather than plush. Mme Corpet used to teach English. Evening meals are expensive but restaurants nearby include her son's, L'Homard, at St-Laurent. Minutes from Vierville beach.

Directions 16 km NW of Bayeux. Take N 13; turn left on D 30 for Aignerville. Signposted.

❖ 14710 Aignerville **Tel** 31 22 51 79 **Fax** 31 22 75 99 **Rooms** 8 **Prices** FFFF **Evening meal** by request **Credit Cards** V **Children** yes **Disabled** no **Pets** yes **Closed** Jan, Feb **Languages** English, Italian **Proprietors** Francine and Yves Corpet

Ardevon, by Mont-St-Michel

La Jacotière

Mont-St-Michel dominates the view from the garden of this plain stone house in the flat meadows south of France's national treasure. The Braults are an energetic young couple who renovated one wing of their home in 1993. French windows lead to the tiled, bare sitting-room/dining-room. The peach-coloured bedrooms upstairs are plain and practical. A useful stopover rather than a place to settle in and stay.

Directions 2 km S of Mont-St-Michel; a short drive along the D 275 coastal lane.

❖ 50170 Ardevon **Tel** 33 60 22 94 **Rooms** 5 **Prices** FF **Evening Meal** no **Credit Cards** no **Children** yes **Disabled** no **Pets** no **Closed** never **Languages** English **Proprietors** Claudine and Gilbert Brault

Asnières-sur-Vègre, SW of Le Mans

Manoir des Claies

On the outskirts of one of the prettiest villages in Sarthe, Jean Anneron has converted this Maine-style manor house into a small bed-and-breakfast. As yet, the newly furnished rooms are a little clinical. Given time, they will aquire a patina to reflect the age of the building. The welcome, the site alongside the river, and even the handsome, if somewhat precarious, staircase have all produced encouraging reports.

Directions 45 km SW of Le Mans. Take the A 81 W; take Exit 1 S on D 4. Go left to Asnières-sur-Vègre.

❖ 72430 Asnières-sur-Vègre **Tel** 43 92 40 50 **Rooms** 2
Prices FFF **Evening meal** no **Credit Cards** no **Children** yes
Disabled no **Pets** no **Closed** weekdays, Nov to March
Languages English **Proprietor** Jean Anneron

Blacqueville, NW of Rouen

Domaine de la Fauconnerie

The busy riding stables are the big attraction at this farm where both parents and children are the hosts. The main house is a fine 17thC building overlooking an apple orchard-cum-garden. Inside, the exposed beams, offset by cream walls and light floral fabrics, give rooms a bright welcoming look that contrasts with the old-fashioned atmosphere in so many Norman homes. The Mignots also run a cheerful *ferme auberge*. Ideal for family holidays.

Directions 18 km NW of Rouen. Take N 15. Turn left on D 22 via Bouville. Well signposted in village.

❖ La Fauconnerie, 76190 Blacqueville **Tel** 35 92 68 08 **Rooms** 5
Prices FF **Evening meal** by request **Credit Cards** no
Children yes **Disabled** no **Pets** yes **Closed** never
Languages some English **Proprietors** René and Annie Mignot
and children

Boncourt, E of Evreux

5 rue Divette

M Beghini bought the old farm 30 years ago but only recently overhauled and renovated the *grange* (barn) himself to provide five comfortable bedrooms complete with beams and private entrances and terraces. Opened in 1991, it is only 15 km away from Monet's house in Giverny and only one hour from Paris by train from Evreux. Brigitte Beghini no longer offers an evening meal since there are several restaurants nearby. Excellent value.

Directions 8 km E of Evreux. Take N 13. Turn left on D 534 opposite grain silo at Caillouet. Follow signs in Boncourt.

❖ 5 rue Divette, 27120 Boncourt **Tel** 32 36 92 44 **Rooms** 5 **Prices** FF **Evening meal** no **Credit Cards** no **Children** no **Disabled** no **Pets** no **Closed** never **Languages** French only **Proprietors** M and Mme Beghini

Bonnebosq, NW of Lisieux

Manoir du Champ Versant

In the heart of cider country, this typical Norman house is post-card-pretty with its half-timbering, red tiled roof and checker-board of brick and stone. In the family for four centuries, it is well-maintained, with a working farm and a small crafts shop selling local paintings, pottery and silk scarves. Guests eat breakfast in a panelled, beamed dining-room crammed with antique furniture. Bedrooms are equally attractive. Value for money.

Directions 20 km NW of Lisieux. Take D 45; left on D 16 to village. Signposted.

❖ 14340 Bonnebosq **Tel** 31 65 11 07 **Rooms** 2 **Prices** FF **Evening meal** no **Credit Cards** no **Children** yes **Disabled** no **Pets** no **Closed** Nov to March **Languages** some English **Proprietor** Marcel Letrésor

Bosc-Roger-s/-Buchy, W of Forges-l.-Eaux

Le Château

Katia Préterre is the dynamic owner of this red-brick country house strategically placed within reach of Dieppe and Rouen. Not surprisingly, it is important to reserve well in advance at this flourishing bed-and-breakfast. Situated in the heart of a village, there is an adequate restaurant nearby in Buchy. The interior has contemporary colours and furniture with high standards of comfort and cleanliness. Some guests bring their horses.
Directions 15 km W of Forges-les-Eaux. Take D 919 to village. Clearly signposted.

❖ place de l'Eglise, 76750 Bosc-Roger-sur-Buchy
Tel 35 34 29 70 **Rooms** 4 **Prices** FFF **Evening meal** no
Credit Cards no **Children** yes **Disabled** no **Pets** yes **Closed** Feb
Languages English **Proprietors** M and Mme Préterre-Rieux

Brélidy, N of Guingamp

Château de Brélidy

This is a strange combination: a 16thC château with hotel rooms on one floor, *chambres d'hôtes* above. Deep in the country, the fortified manor is in well-kept grounds and has a modern glass, wood and stone extension. The small, comfortable bedrooms are named after flowers. Breakfast is at separate tables in an atmospheric room with tapestries on the walls, a suit of armour and high-backed chairs. Odd collectables scattered around. Expensive.
Directions 18 km N of Guingamp. Take D 767 to Bégard; D 15 to village.

❖ 22140 Brélidy **Tel** 96 95 69 38 **Fax** 96 95 18 03 **Rooms** 4
Prices FFF **Evening meal** by request **Credit Cards** DC V
Children yes **Disabled** yes **Pets** yes **Closed** never; telephone in winter **Languages** English **Proprietor** Pierre Yoncourt

Bretteville-sur-Laize, S of Caen

Château des Riffets

M Cantel jokes that he weighs guests on arrival and on departure because of his wife's traditional and delicious Norman dishes. Bedrooms overlook the pretty park and are particularly grand: one has his grandmother's wedding bed. Bathrooms are large and well-equipped with American-style showers. With a history back to William the Conqueror plus contemporary elegance, this is exceptional value. Sauna, Turkish bath and swimming-pool.

Directions 17 km S of Caen. Take N 158; turn right on D 23, D 235. Signposted at village.

❖ 14680 Bretteville-sur-Laize **Tel** 31 23 53 21 **Rooms** 4 **Prices** FFF **Evening meal** by request **Credit Cards** no **Children** yes **Disabled** no **Pets** no **Closed** never **Languages** English, German **Proprietors** Anne-Marie and Alain Cantel

S of Carantec

Manoir de Kervézec

Look to the sea from the impressive balustraded stone terrace of this prim house where surrounding trees and artichoke fields ensure peace and privacy. Anne Bohic, a well-seasoned traveller, has decorated the high-ceilinged downstairs rooms with taste: antiques, leather-bound books, paintings, copper pans and dried flowers. By contrast, bedrooms are plain but comfortable, with small bathrooms. Breakfast, served on pretty china and tablecloths, is traditional.

Directions 1 km S of Carantec. Turn right at town limit. Signposted.

❖ 29660 Carantec **Tel** 98 67 00 26 **Rooms** 6 **Prices** FF **Evening meal** no **Credit Cards** no **Children** yes **Disabled** no **Pets** yes **Closed** never **Languages** English **Proprietor** Anne Bohic

Kerguéarec

Inland among the famous megalithic stones, a low, white, modern home stands by a fast but not too busy road. The garden is well-kept with hedges, walls and plastic green netting giving privacy. With beamed ceilings and tiled floors, the furnishing indoors is old-fashioned, but the welcome cheerful. One of the hosts smokes. A separate kitchen, available for guests, is a boon for families. The price of the cheaper bedrooms reflects their cramped size.

Directions 3 km N of Carnac. Take D 186 for Auray. Look for signs near Les Quatre Chemins.

❖ 56340 Carnac **Tel** 97 56 81 16 **Rooms** 5 **Prices** FF
Evening meal no **Credit Cards** no **Children** yes **Disabled** no
Pets no **Closed** mid-Nov to mid-March **Languages** French only
Proprietor Martine Brient

Caudebec-en-Caux

Cavée St-Léger

The evocative abbeys of Jumièges and St-Wandrille are minutes away from this attractive base for exploring the Seine Valley. The Villamaux family, who really enjoy having guests, have converted a barn into bedrooms: one sleeps four. The large garden with fruit trees gives children space to work off energy after a day's sightseeing. Guests can use the barbecue or prepare their own picnics and evening meals in the kitchen. Sitting-room with television.

Directions rue de la République is the main street of Caudebec, the D 131. The house is opposite the school.

❖ 68 rue de la République, 76490 Caudebec-en-Caux
Tel 35 96 10 15 **Rooms** 3 **Prices** FF **Evening meal** no
Credit Cards no **Children** yes **Disabled** no **Pets** yes **Closed** never
Languages English **Proprietors** Hubert and Christiane
Villamaux

Caumont-L'Eventé, SW of Caen

Le Relais

'Vive les Boullots' was one guest's comment on the lively couple whose luxurious stone house has a garden and swimming-pool. He teaches riding, she teaches sculpting. The sitting-room has a stone floor; the dining-room has beams, copper pans, a huge open fire-place and a long table. The bedrooms have considerable charac-ter: wooden floors, lace curtains, leather books and antiques. A separate cottage is suitable for families.

Directions 37 km SW of Caen. Take D 9 to Caumont; turn right on D 28 for Balleroy. House 300 m on left.

❖ 19 rue Thiers, 14240 Caumont-L'Eventé **Tel** 31 77 47 85
Rooms 3 **Prices** FF **Evening meal** by request **Credit Cards** no
Children yes **Disabled** no **Pets** no **Closed** never
Languages English **Proprietors** Claude and J-Paule Boullot

Chartres

Riverside

The husband is French, his wife is Irish and their home is an appealing mixture of old-world charm and modern convenience. Open for ten years, the 19thC house is surrounded by trees, bush-es and flowers. Inside are antiques and hardwood floors, yet rooms are airy. The dining-room has a view over the river. Bedrooms have antique wardrobes but not all rooms enjoy private facilities. Prices are reasonable.

Directions off place Morard, by the river on SE side of the old city. Well- signposted on boulevard Clemenceau.

❖ 1 boulevard Clemenceau, 28000 Chartres **Tel** 37 35 60 32
Rooms 3 **Prices** FF **Evening meal** no **Credit Cards** no
Children yes **Disabled** no **Pets** yes **Closed** never
Languages English **Proprietors** Jean and Anne Borreye

Cherrueix, W of Mont-St-Michel

La Croix Galliot

Handy for exploring Mont-St-Michel and therefore geared to brief stays. All is tidy: the garden, tarmac driveway, and the house itself. Even the geraniums in terracotta pots are lined up like soldiers on parade. Somewhat hotel-like, with identical bedrooms, wood furniture, plain bed-linen and dark pink bathrooms. The dining-room has a small table, tiled floor, leather sofa and more plain, wood furniture. Thank goodness the owners are friendly.
Directions 20 km W of Mont-St-Michel. Take D 976 S, then D 797. At St-Broladre, left on D 80; right on D 85. Follow signs.

❖ 35120 Cherrueix **Tel** 99 48 90 44 **Rooms** 5 **Prices** FF
Evening meal no **Credit Cards** no **Children** yes **Disabled** no
Pets no **Closed** never **Languages** some English
Proprietors Michel and Marie-France Taillebois

Cherrueix, W of Mont-St-Michel

La Hamelinais

A pretty farmhouse, offering bed-and-breakfast since 1980, has rustic bedrooms that are comfortable enough with crisp white linen on solid wood beds. The split-level rooms are attractive. The plain sitting-room has a massive stone fireplace and big leather armchairs or sofa. The owners are willing to please, offering breakfasts which include their own apple juice and milk. The garden is large, the smell of the farm unavoidable. Value for money.
Directions 20 km W of Mont-St-Michel. Take D 976 S, D 797. Left on D 85 at Cherrueix. Signs on left.

❖ 35120 Cherrueix **Tel** 99 48 95 26 **Rooms** 4 **Prices** FF
Evening meal no **Credit Cards** no **Children** yes **Disabled** no
Pets no **Closed** never **Languages** English
Proprietors Marie-Madeleine and Jean Glémot

Cherrueix, W of Mont-St-Michel

A la Pichardière

Set in an old farmyard on the edge of Mont-St-Michel Bay, this small summer cottage was renovated recently. The stone fireplaces are impressive but the modern, tile-floored dining-room is somewhat clinical despite red gingham cloths on the small tables at breakfast. A television dominates the sitting-room, though most guests sit out on the brick terrace with its marigolds and caged rabbits. Adequate if unexciting bedrooms; two are split-level.

Directions 20 km W of Mont-St-Michel. D 976 S, D 797 to St-Broladre, then Chapelle Ste-Anne. Few signs.

❖ 172 la Pichardière, 35120 Cherrueix **Tel** 99 48 83 82 or 99 48 93 96 **Fax** 99 02 97 38 **Rooms** 5 **Prices** FF **Evening meal** no **Credit Cards** no **Children** yes **Disabled** no **Pets** no **Closed** Nov to Easter **Languages** French only **Proprietors** André and Louise Philippe

Commana, S of Morlaix

Kerfornédic

Moss on stone walls and wrought-iron cockerels and foxes on the roof ridge lend a romantic quality to this cottage, saved from dereliction some five years ago. The walled garden is crammed with fruit and vegetables. Inside, walls are bright white and dried flowers hang from beams. The ground floor bedrooms are small but pretty, with red-checked bedspreads and fresh flowers in bathrooms. The charming hostess serves Arrée cheeses at breakfast.

Directions 25 km S of Morlaix. Not in Commana. Take D 785, D 764 to Commana, D 130 to St-Cadou. House 4 km on left.

❖ 29450 Commana **Tel** 98 78 06 26 **Rooms** 2 **Prices** FF **Evening meal** no **Credit Cards** no **Children** yes **Disabled** no **Pets** no **Closed** never **Languages** French only **Proprietors** Danielle and Michel Le Signor

La Couyère, SE of Rennes

La Tremblais

The owner of this long, low farmhouse is an interior designer and her skill shows, from the sheepskin on a rocking chair to lavender-scented sheets. The larger bedroom has stone walls, beams, a wood-burning fireplace, plus a sofa and a double bed on a mezzanine floor up an open wooden staircase. Claudine is a fine cook, grilling salmon and beef over the fire and making crêpes. Champagne and candles on request.

Directions 30 km SE of Rennes. Take D 163 for La Couyère; turn sharp left on D 92 to La Tremblais. Signposted.

❖ La Couyère, 35320 Le Sel-de-Bretagne **Tel** 99 43 14 39
Rooms 2 **Prices** FF **Evening meal** by request **Credit Cards** no
Children yes **Disabled** no **Pets** no **Closed** never
Languages English, Spanish **Proprietors** Claudine and Raymond Gomis

Crouttes, W of Vimoutiers

Prieuré St-Michel

This former Benedictine priory, deep in the country near the cheese town of Vimoutiers and the village of Camembert, has been turned into a cultural centre, attracting intellectuals from all over France for conferences and seminars. While the bedrooms are well-kept, the welcome is somewhat institutional. Worth staying to enjoy the atmosphere of this listed historic monument. In summer, concerts and art exhibitions.

Directions Crouttes is a hamlet 4 km W of Vimoutiers off D 916. Follow signposts to Prieuré beyond Crouttes on D 218.

❖ 61120 Crouttes, near Vimoutiers **Tel** 33 39 15 15
Fax 33 36 15 16 **Rooms** 4 **Prices** FFFF **Evening meal** no
Credit Cards V **Children** yes **Disabled** no **Pets** yes **Closed** Feb, Mar **Languages** English, German, Spanish **Proprietors** Pierre and Anne Chahine

Dol-de-Bretagne

L'Aunay-Bégasse

A fine example of a working farm some 7 km from the coast, complete with smells, sounds and animals. The farmer's jolly wife provides a reasonably priced evening meal. The rustic but comfortable bedrooms have huge oak beds, beamed ceilings, homely ornaments. Breakfast is served at a long table with a lace cloth. Outside, a swing hangs from a chestnut tree. No wonder the visitor's book is full of praise for this corner of rural France.
Directions 1 km from middle of Dol-de-Bretagne, SW towards Baguer-Morvan. Near Lycée Alphonse Pelée.

❖ 35120 Dol-de-Bretagne **Tel** 99 48 16 93 **Fax** 99 02 97 38
Rooms 3 **Prices** FF **Evening meal** by request **Credit Cards** no
Children yes **Disabled** no **Pets** no **Closed** never
Languages French only **Proprietors** Maryvonne and Alain Roncier

SW of Dol-de-Bretagne

Ferme-Manoir d'Halouze

A table long enough to seat 22 for dinner dominates the huge dining-room with its high ceiling and wooden beams. The owners enjoy the *table d'hôte* side of the business, joining guests for dinners of tomato and parsley soup, pork with honey and tomatoes, rice with smoked salmon or cheese soufflé. Some bedrooms in the delightful stone house have four-poster beds, lace curtains; we like the room in the tower. Excellent value for money.
Directions 3 km SW of Dol-de-Bretagne. Take N 176, then D 119 for Baguer-Morvan. Clearly signposted on right.

❖ 35120 Dol-de-Bretagne **Tel** 99 48 07 46 **Rooms** 6 **Prices** FF
Evening meal by request **Credit Cards** no **Children** yes
Disabled no **Pets** yes **Closed** mid-Nov to mid-Feb
Languages English, Spanish **Proprietors** Myriam Mathias and Pascal Jubault

Manoir de Kervent

The Lefloch house is a popular place to stay on the coast, although our inspector was not impressed by the small yapping dog. A rough track leads through well-kept gardens with a palm tree and pampas grass to the creeper-covered stone house. The bedrooms and downstairs rooms are comfortable rather than luxurious with attractive furniture and lace curtains at the windows. Visitors return because the hostess is so pleasant.

Directions 2 km SW of Douarnenez. Take D 765. Look for signs on the right on edge of town.

❖ Pouldavid, 29100 Douarnenez **Tel** 98 92 04 90 **Rooms** 3 **Prices** FF **Evening meal** no **Credit Cards** no **Children** yes **Disabled** no **Pets** yes **Closed** never **Languages** French only **Proprietor** Marie-Paule Lefloch

Equemauville, S of Honfleur

La Ferme Chevallier

More thatch, more half-timbering, more apple trees at this 17thC house which even has a thatched, half-timbered well outside. The bedrooms, by contrast, have been completely modernised so are clean, comfortable, with firm new beds but lack the character of the old house. Breakfast in the dining-room is a wide array of cheeses and jams, yoghurts and breads. Useful for an overnight stay. Peaceful. Restaurant 1 km. Well-priced for families.

Directions 8 km S of Honfleur. Take D 180, D 144 through Gonneville. Right on D 289. House on left before Equemauville.

❖ 14600 Equemauville **Tel** 31 89 18 14 **Rooms** 5 **Prices** FF **Evening meal** no **Credit Cards** no **Children** yes **Disabled** yes **Pets** yes **Closed** never **Languages** some English **Proprietors** Françoise and Yves Grégoire

Ermenouville, S of St-Valery

Château du Mesnil-Geoffroy

The owners have worked to make this imposing château as prestigious as it was in the 18thC. Garden lovers admire Le Nôtre's landscaping and the hornbeam-hedge maze. Inside, carved wood in the downstairs rooms plus antiques in the bedrooms are matched by modern comforts. The romantic Marquis de Cany room has a Polish-style canopy bed. Despite the grandeur, the hosts are welcoming and keen to promote the region.

Directions 10 km S of St-Valery-en-Caux. Take D 20, left on D 108. Signposted on left in Ermenouville.

❖ 76740 Ermenouville **Tel** 35 57 12 77 **Fax** 35 57 10 24
Rooms 7 **Prices** FFFF **Evening meal** by request **Credit Cards** no
Children yes **Disabled** no **Pets** no **Closed** never; telephone in
winter **Languages** English **Proprietors** Dr and Mme Kayali

Erquy

Les Bruyères

The owners built this pink stone 'imitation farmhouse' at the end of the 1980s and one bedroom is specially adapted for wheelchair access. Furnishings, however, are bland: modern beds and lights, black chairs and posters on the walls. Family suites have two bedrooms linked by a bathroom. Guests may use the kitchen to cook their own dinner. Although lacking in atmosphere and style, we appreciate the practicality here which families often require.

Directions 1 km E of Erquy. Follow signs to Les Hôpitaux. Les Bruyères signposted.

❖ Les Ruaux, 22430 Erquy **Tel** 96 72 31 59 **Rooms** 3 **Prices** FF
Evening meal no **Credit Cards** no **Children** yes **Disabled** yes
Pets no **Closed** never **Languages** English **Proprietor** Aline
Dutemple

La Ferté-Vidame, NW of Chartres

Manoir de la Motte

A park with huge trees and fields surrounds the manoir which is less grand than a château but more imposing than an ordinary house. One bedroom has an Empire bed with pretty yellow bed-curtains in a reproduction 18thC pattern, a marble fireplace and a modern bathroom with an array of perfumes to try. Breakfast includes cereals, yoghurts, croissants, brioches, fresh fruit and six different jams. Beware: the wooden stairs can be slippery.

Directions 50 km NW of Chartres. Take D 24 to Senonches, then D 941 to La Ferté. La Motte is l.5 km beyond village.

❖ 28340 La Ferté-Vidame **Tel** 37 37 51 69 **Fax** 37 37 51 56
Rooms 2 **Prices** FFF **Evening meal** by request **Credit Cards** no
Children yes **Disabled** no **Pets** yes **Closed** never
Languages English, German **Proprietors** Anne and Jean-Pierre Jallot

Gonneville-sur-Scie, S of Dieppe

Domaine de Champdieu

Denis Buquet has taken bed-and-breakfast to a superior plane that leaves some guests amazed, and others aghast. The former love the Norman half-timbering of the 17thC main house, the pretty, if functional, bedrooms in the 19thC guest house and the gourmet dinners by candle-light that range from expensive to once-in-a-life-time experiences, featuring game and champagne. The latter don't like the formality and show.

Directions 20 km S of Dieppe, just E of the N 27. Follow signs on the D 203.

❖ Les Hameaux, 76590 Gonneville-sur-Scie **Tel** 35 32 66 82
Rooms 6 **Prices** FFFF **Evening meal** by request **Credit Cards** AE DC MC V **Children** no **Disabled** no **Pets** no **Closed** never
Languages English, Spanish **Proprietor** Denis Buquet

Hébécrevon, W of St-Lô

Château de la Roque

Former cycling champion Raymond Delisle has transferred his professionalism to the 14thC manor house whose driveway tends to be full of British cars. We were disappointed by the quality of the evening meal in the beamed, echoing refectory. Moreover, the atmosphere seems more 'small hotel' than 'bed-and-breakfast'. The hosts are business-like but friendly; the bedrooms have television and telephone; the bathrooms have soaps and shampoo.
Directions 5 km W of St-Lô. Take D 900; go through Hébécrevon. House on left at crossroad with D 77.

❖ 50180 Hébécrevon **Tel** 33 57 33 20 **Fax** 33 57 51 20 **Rooms** 5
Prices FF **Evening meal** by request **Credit Cards** no
Children yes **Disabled** no **Pets** yes **Closed** never
Languages English **Proprietors** Raymond and Mireille Delisle

Herbignac, NW of St-Nazaire

Château de Coët-Caret

Lawns lead to a lake; stone steps climb to the front door of this 19thC manor house where cars are parked out of sight, on one side. The owner is an expert in flower arrangement and her sense of colour and design shows. The bedrooms are particularly pretty: perhaps with cream walls, matching blue-patterned curtains, bed-spread and chairs. Quality antiques. Dinner seems expensive but aperitifs and wines are included with the regional seafood dishes.
Directions 23 km NW of St-Nazaire. Take D 99, D 47 via St-Lyphard. House on left before Herbignac.

❖ 44410 Herbignac **Tel** 40 91 41 20 **Fax** 40 91 37 46 **Rooms** 3
Prices FFF **Evening meal** by request **Credit Cards** no
Children no **Disabled** no **Pets** no **Closed** never
Languages English, Spanish **Proprietors** M and Mme de la Monneraye

Mesnières-en-Bray, SE of Dieppe

Le Rambure

The Gallaghers run a language school from their converted farm-house half-an-hour from Dieppe. Their home is on one side of the courtyard, guest rooms are opposite, in what was the cowshed. Above a huge sitting-room, bedrooms have exposed beams and views of the Loire-like château of Mesnières. Dinner is a relaxed four-course affair with the hosts and a free glass of home-made Calvados. Attractive value for money.

Directions 32 km SE of Dieppe. Take D 1 to Mesnières. Turn right on D 97 towards Fresles. Well signposted.

❖ 76270 Mesnières-en-Bray **Tel** 35 94 14 13 **Rooms** 5 **Prices** FF **Evening meal** yes **Credit Cards** no **Children** yes **Disabled** no **Pets** yes **Closed** never **Languages** English **Proprietors** Kate and Oliver Gallagher

Le Mesnil-Rogues, E of Granville

Le Verger

The Bennetts rescued a dilapidated farmhouse, then opened for bed-and-breakfast in 1993. The lawn, gardens and apple orchards are immaculate; a conservatory has been added. The pretty bed-rooms have a mixture of old and new furniture; bathrooms are small but fresh. The hosts share their English-style sitting-room and join guests for breakfast in the dining-room with its beams, stone fireplace, and long table. In a village; inn nearby.

Directions 20 km E of Granville. Take D 924; left on D 7. Follow signs in village.

❖ Le Mesnil-Rogues, 50450 Gavray **Tel** 33 90 19 20 **Rooms** 4 **Prices** FF **Evening meal** no **Credit Cards** no **Children** yes **Disabled** no **Pets** yes **Closed** never **Languages** English, Spanish **Proprietors** Gordon and Dee Bennett

Mézangers, NW of Evron

Le Cruchet

The helpful owners have restored this 400-year-old town house with considerable taste, making it an unpretentious stopover in the Mayenne countryside The ground floor bedroom is small with both a double bed and a single. Up a stone spiral staircase is the much larger second bedroom, with rugs on the stone floor. Although there is central heating, it felt somewhat chilly on an autumn visit. A restaurant is within walking distance.

Directions 5 km NW of Evron. Take D 7 for Mayenne. Clearly marked in centre of Mézangers

❖ 53600 Mézangers **Tel** 43 90 65 55 **Rooms** 2 **Prices** FF
Evening meal no **Credit Cards** no **Children** yes **Disabled** no
Pets yes **Closed** never; telephone in winter **Languages** some
English, Spanish **Proprietors** Marie-Thérèse and Léopold Nay

Montreuil-en-Auge, E of Caen

Auberge de la Route du Cidre

In the heart of Normandy's best-known cider area, this is more of a restaurant-with-rooms, since the family's main business is the surprisingly large, half-timbered *auberge*. Three jolly dining-rooms attract cyclists and day-trippers who order *tarte camembert*, duck, *gâteau normand*, crêpes and waffles. The bedrooms are somewhat disappointing: clean but plain, so geared more to overnights rather than long stays. Swings, mini-golf for children.

Directions 33 km E of Caen. Take N 13, D 5, D 101 to Cambremer. House on D 101 between Cambremer and Montreuil.

❖ 14340 Cambremer **Tel and Fax** 31 63 12 27 **Rooms** 4
Prices FF **Evening meal** in *auberge* **Credit Cards** no **Children** yes
Disabled no **Pets** yes **Closed** Jan, Feb **Languages** some English
Proprietors Gesbert family

Moulicent, E of Mortagne-au-P.

La Grande Noë

Don't be put off by the grand Adam-style entrance hall. Although the de Longcamp family have lived here for 500 years, they are quite down-to-earth. The rooms with their antique furniture have recently been redecorated. As M de Longcamp also runs a Camembert factory, evening meals in the 18thC dining-room always finish with a properly ripened cheese.
Directions 18 km E of Mortagne-au-Perche. Take D 8 to Longny-au-Perche. Then N on D 918 to les Epasses. Turn E on D 289 for Moulicent. Château is on right, before village.

❖ 61290 Moulicent **Tel** 33 73 63 30 **Fax** 33 83 62 92
Rooms 3 **Prices** FFF-FFFF **Evening meal** by request
Credit Cards AE DC MC V **Children** yes **Disabled** no **Pets** yes
Closed never **Languages** English, Spanish **Proprietors** M and Mme Jacques de Longcamp

Neuvy-en-Champagne, NW of Le Mans

Château de la Renaudière

Dating from the 15thC and 17thC, the château has steep roofs, mansard windows and turrets. Bedrooms are very much like family spare rooms, "but that's what I like about staying in a bed-and-breakfast," one guest told us. Each room has an adjoining children's room. The family offers to eat with you or to leave you in peace, a clear choice that other châteaux could copy. Imperative to telephone ahead of time.
Directions 20 km NW of Le Mans. N 157 W to Coulans; then D 88 N towards Conlie. Château just past St-Julien-le-Pauvre on right.

❖ 72240 Neuvy-en-Champagne **Tel** 43 20 71 09 **Rooms** 4
Prices FFFF **Evening meal** by request **Credit Cards** no
Children yes **Disabled** no **Pets** yes **Closed** Nov to April
Languages English **Proprietors** Marquis and Marquise de Mascureau

Plélo, E of Guingamp

Au Char à Bancs

The enterprising owners also run the nearby *ferme auberge* and a museum of local life. Creeper covers the building where bedrooms have themes such as clocks, music or birds. Les Oiseaux has painted bird cages, a single brass bed, a pretty blue and white double bed, huge antique furniture and an old china jug and bowl. Bathrooms are small but modern. With swings, an adventure playground, horses and a stream, children are happy here. Opened in 1990.

Directions 15 km E of Guingamp. Take N 12, exit at Châtelaudren. Plélo is 4 km NE; house NW of village, past *ferme auberge*.

❖ Moulin de la Ville Geffroy, 22170 Plélo **Tel** 96 74 13 63
Rooms 4 **Prices** FFF **Evening meal** at *ferme auberge*
Credit Cards V **Children** yes **Disabled** no **Pets** no
Closed never **Languages** English, German, Spanish
Proprietors Lamour family

Pléneuf-Val-André, E of le Val-André

Ferme du Pré-Mancel

Three grey stone buildings cluster round a gravelled courtyard in a rural setting minutes from the sea and clean beaches. Open only since 1990, guests are in a separate building from the hosts. Bedrooms have modern pine furniture, small bathrooms, some low ceilings. The dining-room is big, bare and uncomfortable though pretty china and tablecloths help to brighten breakfast. The attractive garden and reasonable prices make this useful for families on a budget.

Directions 1 km E of le Val-André. Take D 786. Well signposted.

❖ 22370 Pléneuf-Val-André **Tel** 96 72 95 12 **Rooms** 5
Prices FF **Evening meal** no **Credit Cards** no **Children** yes
Disabled yes **Pets** yes **Closed** never **Languages** English
Proprietor Yvette Rouinvy

Plougonven, SE of Morlaix

La Grange de Coatelan

A lively young couple own this restored barn that is a welcome contrast to the often gloomy granite mansions of Brittany. The bedrooms, above a crêperie, are decorated in bright colours with bold modern paintings by the owner, a professional artist. Breakfast is hearty with *far* or *gâteau breton*; dinner might include the famous *kig-ha-fars*, a meat stew with buckwheat dumplings. Reasonably priced, informal, deep in the country.

Directions 12 km SE of Morlaix. Take D 9 to village. Well # signposted.

❖ 29640 Plougonven **Tel** 98 72 60 16 **Rooms** 2 **Prices** FF
Evening meal by request **Credit Cards** V **Children** yes
Disabled no **Pets** no **Closed** mid-Nov to Easter
Languages English **Proprietors** Charlick and Yolande de Ternay

Plougrescant, N of Tréguier

Kernevez

M Janvier worked at sea, so his wife wanted to keep busy. Now this bubbly, motherly lady is a 20-year veteran of the business. Popular with walkers exploring this remote, rugged coastline, the house is a home-from-home. One bedroom has pine floor boards, busy green and yellow wallpaper that also covers the ceiling, pretty white bed-linen and a view of the village. Another has an old writing desk, old books and television. A third looks to the sea. Well priced.

Directions 8 km N of Tréguier. Take D 8. Near church with crooked spire.

❖ route du Gouffre, 22820 Plougrescant **Tel** 96 92 52 67
Rooms 3 **Prices** FF **Evening meal** no **Credit Cards** no
Children yes **Disabled** no **Pets** no **Closed** never
Languages English, Breton **Proprietor** Marie-Claude Janvier

Manoir de Kergrec'h

The 18thC Breton manor house, built of local pink granite and full of antiques, is run by a young couple. A monumental staircase leads to the recently redecorated bedrooms. All overlook the park and, beyond that, the sea. Breakfast in Brittany is a serious affair and crêpes are almost always served in the elegant dining-room. Although the owner is a busy farmer, his wife advises on the best spots to explore on the rugged coast.

Directions 7 km N of Tréguier. Take D 8 to village. Turn right after chapel. Manoir in 800 m.

❖ Kergrec'h, 22820 Plougrescant **Tel** 96 92 56 06 **Fax** 96 92 51 27 **Rooms** 5 **Prices** FFF **Evening meal** by request **Credit Cards** no **Children** yes **Disabled** no **Pets** yes **Closed** never **Languages** English **Proprietors** Vicomte and Vicomtesse de Roquefeuil

Château de Kermezen

This big, solid, stone 17thC château sits in a peaceful valley, not far from Brittany's Pink Granite Coast. Although the Kermel family has been in residence for five centuries, the current Comtesse is known as a 'colourful character', both outgoing and friendly. The Cockerels (Aux Coqs) is the most popular of the bedrooms; breakfast can be brought to you there. But who would want to miss the experience of eating in the grand dining-room?

Directions Pommerit-Jaudy is 23 km NW of Guingamp on the D 8. Turn left at traffic lights in Pommerit-Jaudy, Château in 2 km.

❖ 22450 Pommerit-Jaudy **Tel** 96 91 35 75 **Rooms** 5 **Prices** FFF-FFFF **Evening meal** no **Credit Cards** V **Children** yes **Disabled** no **Pets** yes **Closed** Christmas **Languages** English **Proprietors** Comte and Comtesse de Kermel

Port Manech, S of Pont-Aven

Kérambris

The owner converted a stone barn "to preserve my heritage", but several ramshackle farm buildings remain. Kittens cavort on wood-piles and farm machinery. With fields and apple orchards, this is a quiet spot five minutes' walk from the sea. Despite a decade in the business, Yveline is still shy but friendly. We like the smell of breakfast *crêpes* and the beautiful gilded furniture in the dining-room but must emphasise that bathrooms are very simple.

Directions 10 km S of Pont-Aven. Take D 77 via Névez. House signposted before village on right.

❖ 29920 Port Manech-Névez **Tel** 96 06 83 82 **Rooms** 4 **Prices** FF
Evening meal no **Credit Cards** no **Children** yes **Disabled** no
Pets no **Closed** never **Languages** English **Proprietor** Yveline Gourlaouen

Prat, NW of Guingamp

Manoir de Coadelan

This impressive fortified manor house has been in the family for more than three centuries but today's guests stay in the converted barn next door. Bedrooms are bright, modern and practical with geometric patterns on curtains and bedspreads. The English-style gardens are beautiful, with two lakes, many trees and ten donkeys. Comfortable and unpretentious, it is a pity rooms aren't in the manor itself but you can have a free guided tour.

Directions 22 km NW of Guingamp. Take D 767. Right on D 35. Right on D 21. House 2 km beyond village. Follow signs.

❖ 22140 Prat **Tel** 96 47 00 60 **Rooms** 6 **Prices** FF
Evening meal no **Credit Cards** no **Children** yes **Disabled** yes
Pets no **Closed** never **Languages** French only
Proprietors M and Mme Riou

Rochefort-en-Terre, E of Vannes

Château de Talhouët

Impressive inside and out: the long driveway leads past tall trees to a three-storey stone mansion with wood panelling, tapestries, leather furniture and painted beams. The owner's excellent taste combines formality with comfort. The spacious bedrooms have massive fireplaces, armchairs and tables, and Laura Ashley-style curtains and bedspreads. Modern bathrooms. Very expensive meals. A 'sumptuous but worthwhile luxury' – if you can afford it.
Directions 32 km E of Vannes. Take N 166, D 775. Turn left on D 777 to Rochefort-en-Terre; left again on D 774. Château on left.

❖ Pluherlin, 56220 Rochefort-en-Terre **Tel** 97 43 34 72
Fax 97 43 35 04 **Rooms** 8 **Prices** FFFF **Evening meal** by request
Credit Cards AE V **Children** yes **Disabled** no **Pets** yes
Closed never **Languages** English **Proprietor** Jean-Pol Soulaine

Rouen, city centre

45 rue aux Ours

Just a few steps from the cathedral is the Aulnays' 300-year-old half-timbered home, where Philippe's grandfather's name is picked out in plaster above the windows. Inside are antiques and sculptures, original wood floors, high ceilings with heavy beams and paintings on the walls. There is even a Gauguin connection. Somewhat sombre, this would be museum-like were it not for the Aulnays' enthusiasm. Two bedrooms share a WC.
Directions rue aux Ours runs W off the square in front of the cathedral.

❖ 45 rue aux Ours, 76000 Rouen **Tel** 35 70 99 68 **Rooms** 4
Prices FF **Evening meal** no **Credit Cards** no **Children** yes
Disabled no **Pets** yes **Closed** never; telephone in winter
Languages German **Proprietors** Annick and Philippe Aulnay

Roz-s/-Couesnon, NW of Pontorson

Le Val St-Revert

The owner is a bubbly, welcoming hostess who offered free bed-and-breakfast in 1990 just to meet people. Now her enthusiasm draws paying visitors from all over the world. Mont-St-Michel is visible from her garden, silhouetted against the sky. The bedrooms all have new bed-linen, some have brass bedsteads and luxurious floral bedspreads. The showers are tiny but clean. Seafood restaurant within walking distance.

Directions No signs, so hard to find. Telephone. 6 km NW of Pontorson. Take D 797, turn left to Val St-Revert before Roz.

❖ 35610 Roz-sur-Couesnon **Tel** 99 80 27 85 **Rooms** 5 **Prices** FF **Evening meal** no **Credit Cards** no **Children** yes **Disabled** yes **Pets** yes **Closed** never **Languages** English **Proprietor** Hélène Gillet

St-Aubin-sur-Scie, S of Dieppe

Rouxmesnil-le-Haut

The owners try to be more than just an overnight stop near the coast. Bedrooms are in a separate, modernized building at the back of their home where a fully equipped kitchen is next to the sitting-room. The double-bedded room on the ground floor has access for wheelchairs. Upstairs, bedrooms are identical: tiled with modern French furniture, exceptionally clean. Two share a WC. With its garden and table tennis, an enjoyable base for families.

Directions 5 km S of Dieppe. Take D 915. Signposted just beyond outskirts of Dieppe.

❖ D 915, 76550 St-Aubin-sur-Scie **Tel** 35 84 14 89 **Rooms** 5 **Prices** FF **Evening meal** no **Credit Cards** no **Children** yes **Disabled** yes **Pets** no **Closed** never **Languages** some English, German **Proprietors** M and Mme Gérard Lulague

St-Briac-sur-Mer, SW of Dinard

Manoir de la Duchée

Roses climb up the 17thC house surrounded by large oak trees and stone statues in the garden. The family have lived here for decades but only opened in 1992 so a homey feeling remains. An open fireplace burns logs in the hall, old dolls and antiques add to the atmosphere, which some may think a bit cluttered. The bedrooms are themed: one small room is green, another has poppy designs, a third has purple bedheads and a skylight.

Directions 5 km SW of Dinard. Take D 168. Just past airport, turn right on D 5. House signposted on right.

❖ 35800 St-Briac-sur-Mer **Tel** 99 88 00 02 **Rooms** 5 **Prices** FFF
Evening meal no **Credit Cards** no **Children** yes **Disabled** no
Pets no **Closed** Dec to Feb **Languages** English, German
Proprietor Jean-François Stenou

St-Gatien-des-Bois, S of Honfleur

Ancienne Cidrerie

Another classic thatched, black-and-white Norman cottage. Guests enter via a gate at the end of a long drive. The well-kept garden is pretty in summer with yellow pansies and pink geraniums. Indoors, the owner, a specialist in stress therapy, has a collection of dolls from around the world in a glass showcase. The breakfast-room with a tiled floor, rugs and antique furniture, is attractive. The bedrooms have been renovated recently.

Directions 8 km S of Honfleur. Take D 180, D 144 for Gonneville. Well-signposted on left.

❖14130 St-Gatien-des-Bois **Tel** 31 98 85 62 **Rooms** 2 **Prices** FF
Evening meal no **Credit Cards** no **Children** yes **Disabled** no
Pets yes **Closed** never **Languages** French only **Proprietor** Renée Rufin

St-Georges-de-la-R, SE of Barneville

Manoir de Caillemont

The owner was a flight engineer, so his skill was welcome when our inspector's car broke down at this early-18thC country mansion. Bedrooms are named after the nearby Channel Islands. Jersey and Guernsey have their own sitting-rooms; Ecréhous boasts a wood-burning fireplace. Although these are large rooms, the panelled dining-room is cosy. Heated swimming-pool in the garden. Expensive, but worth it.

Directions 6 km SE of Barneville-Carteret. Take D 903. At St-Georges crossroads, turn left for St-Maurice. First house on left.

❖ 50270 St-Georges-de-la-Rivière **Tel** 33 53 81 16
Fax 33 53 25 66 **Rooms** 3 **Prices** FFFF **Evening meal** no
Credit Cards no **Children** yes **Disabled** yes **Pets** yes
Closed never; telephone in winter **Languages** English
Proprietors M and Mme Coupechoux

St-Hymer, S of Pont-l'Evêque

Le Moulin

'Mme Vallé was up early and had breakfast ready so I could get to the ferry in good time,' reported one British guest who stayed in the restored mill. Her bedroom, with pink and white gingham curtains and bedcovers, was small but attractive. The bathroom was 'good-sized', with plenty of hot water. The welcome may be more restrained than effusive but everything is clean and fresh-looking. An Alsatian is the guard-dog.

Directions 3 km S of Pont-l'Evêque. Take D 48. Look for signs on right, after Pierrefitte-en-Auge.

❖ St-Hymer, 14130 Pont-l'Evêque **Tel** 31 64 23 51 **Rooms** 2
Prices FF **Evening meal** by request **Credit Cards** no **Children** no
Disabled no **Pets** no **Closed** never **Languages** English
Proprietor Mme Françoise Vallé

St-Jean-du-Card., NW of Rouen

La Ferme du Vivier

Prince Rainier of Monaco's connection with this tidy working farm is another story. His tenant-farmers have four bedrooms with television and modern bathrooms plus a proper kitchen in the new, somewhat bare extension. One room has disabled access. The atmospheric dining-room in the old house has a large fireplace, long communal table and a wooden butterchurn converted into a drinks cabinet. Well-priced, suitable for families.

Directions 7 km NW of Rouen. Take N 15. At junction with D 90, turn right for Le Houlme. Signposted on right.

❖ 88 route de Duclair, 76150 St-Jean-du-Cardonnay
Tel 35 33 80 42 **Rooms** 4 **Prices** FF **Evening meal** no
Credit Cards no **Children** yes **Disabled** yes **Pets** no **Closed** never
Languages French only **Proprietors** Marie-Cécile and Jean-Claude Lambert

St-Jouan-des-Guérets, S of St-Malo

Manoir de Blanche Roche

This large, attractive red-brick manor house is, unfortunately, just off a motorway so traffic noise spoils the appeal of sitting in the pleasant walled garden with its palm trees. Parents and daughters help run the business-like operation. Bedrooms are neat and clean but plain: one, the Mont-St-Michel, has a picture of the mount on the wall and a pink bathroom. Breakfast, and the well-priced evening meal, are served at a communal table.

Directions 5 km S of St-Malo. Take N 137 to St-Jouan roundabout. Follow signs back to St-Malo and take first road on right.

❖ 35430 St-Jouan-des-Guérets **Tel** 99 82 47 47 **Rooms** 5
Prices FFF **Evening meal** by request; not in July, Aug
Credit Cards no **Children** yes **Disabled** no **Pets** no **Closed** mid-Nov to mid-Jan **Languages** English **Proprietor** Magali Mérienne

St-Léger, SE of Granville

Manoir de Vaucelles

With a tree-lined drive, lawns and fields, this is somewhat isolated but there is a comforting old-fashioned feel about the farmhouse where Marie-Thérèse Clouet roasts leg of lamb in the fireplace in front of guests. With its low beams and high-backed, red velvet chairs, the dining-room is a convivial spot. Although bedrooms are rustic, with beams, stone walls and oak beds, skylights in the ceiling make them bright and airy. Value for money.

Directions 12 km SE of Granville. Take D 973, then D 309 towards Abbaye de la Lucerne. Well-signposted in St-Léger.

❖ St-Léger, 50320 La Haye-Pesnel **Tel** 33 51 66 97 **Rooms** 2 **Prices** FF **Evening meal** by request **Credit Cards** no **Children** yes **Disabled** no **Pets** no **Closed** never **Languages** English **Proprietors** Marie-Thérèse and James Clouet

St-Malo

Clermont

Behind the house, a separate building has the bedrooms, each with its own entrance. The look is functional: a tiled floor, lace curtains, a bench, modern wardrobe and paisley bedspread. The shower-rooms are small but clean. We did not like the pictures but approve of the prices. The owner, whose husband was mayor of St-Malo, is kind and motherly. Breakfast is in a homely, large, old-fashioned room. Cars are parked in an open barn.

Directions hard to find. Telephone. 3 km E of St-Malo. Right off D 155, just after Français Libres roundabout. 2 km on left.

❖ 35400 St-Malo **Tel** 99 81 07 69 **Rooms** 5 **Prices** FF **Evening meal** no **Credit Cards** no **Children** yes **Disabled** yes **Pets** yes **Closed** never **Languages** French only **Proprietor** Louise Chopier

E of St-Malo

La Ville Auray

Not to be confused with the nearby Villa Auray le Gué, this stands
in a wooded park in flat cabbage fields. The owner is welcoming,
smiling and helpful. The house itself is not particularly attractive
but prices are reasonable. Steep, narrow stairs lead to bedrooms
which are adequate with modern fittings and television, but low
ceilings. One has a bathroom in the tower with a garish mauve
bath, sink, WC and shower, but towels are fluffy.

Directions 3 km E of St-Malo. At Français Libres roundabout on
outskirts of town, take D 155. House soon signposted on left.

❖ 35400 St-Malo **Tel** 99 81 64 37 **Fax** 99 82 23 27 **Rooms** 4
Prices FF **Evening meal** no **Credit Cards** no **Children** yes
Disabled no **Pets** yes **Closed** never **Languages** English, Spanish
Proprietor Josette Feret

St-Méloir-des-Ondes, S of Cancale

Langavan

Exposed and wind-swept, the house has views over the sea. Dinner
is a bargain even by *table d'hôte* standards and includes produce
from the owners' farm. Although cheerful and friendly, they rarely
have time to eat with guests. Some think the separate tables lend
an impersonal restaurant-like feel, others like the privacy.
Bedrooms are modern with pine furniture and bunk beds in family rooms. No prizes for the decoration.

Directions 5 km S of Cancale. Not in St-Méloir. Take D 76, then D
155. Signposted on left.

❖ 35350 St-Méloir-des-Ondes **Tel** 99 89 22 92 or 99 58 71 37
Rooms 5 **Prices** FF **Evening meal** by request **Credit Cards** no
Children yes **Disabled** yes **Pets** yes **Closed** Nov to Easter
Languages English **Proprietors** Loïc and Sophie Collin

St-Michel-de-Plélan, W of Dinan

La Corbinais

Deep in farming country, but next door to a golf course, the stone cottage has old, moss-covered roof tiles. Although the garden is somewhat scruffy, the rooms look snug. The large dining-room has beams, stone walls, dark antique furniture and plenty of books. The bedrooms are brighter and have modern bathrooms. The evening meal represents particularly fair value. A friendly sheep-dog lives here.

Directions 16 km W of Dinan. Take N 176; turn right, go through Plélan-le-Petit, then D 19 to village. Signposted.

❖ 22980 St-Michel-de-Plélan **Tel** 96 27 64 81 **Rooms** 4
Prices FF **Evening meal** by request **Credit Cards** no
Children yes **Disabled** no **Pets** yes **Closed** never
Languages English **Proprietor** Henri Beaupère

St-Nicolas-de-Pierrepont, N of Lessay

La Ferme de l'Eglise

On the Cotentin Peninsula, an English couple have an attractive stone house with furniture from Britain and France. A Mexican rug adds a splash of colour to one bedroom wall. Another bedroom, right under the roof, has exposed beams, skylights and a view across fields. Breakfast is praised for its freshly squeezed orange juice. With dogs and cats everywhere and bicycles available, families are happy here. Particularly well-priced.

Directions 13 km N of Lessay. Take D 900, D 903. Turn right on D 127 to St-Nicolas. Near church.

❖ Village de l'Eglise, 50250 St-Nicolas-de-Pierrepont **Tel** 33 45 53 40 **Rooms** 2 **Prices** FF **Evening meal** no **Credit Cards** no
Children yes **Disabled** no **Pets** yes **Closed** never
Languages English, German **Proprietors** Jay and Richard Clay

St-Paterne, SE of Alençon

Château de St-Paterne

The owner, who decided to restore his grandparents' dilapidated home, maintains a balance between the formal and informal. At dinner, the family silver, crystal, porcelain and decanters are used but dress is casual, conversation lively. Similarly, some guests stroll down to breakfast at 10 am. Our favourite bedroom, with a painted ceiling, was slept in by King Henri IV and his mistress 400 years ago. A delightful base for exploring an underrated area.

Directions 2 km SE of Alençon. Take D 311 towards St. Paterne (not bypass). Château on right in village.

❖ 72610 St-Paterne **Tel** 33 27 54 71 **Fax** 33 29 16 71 **Rooms** 7 **Prices** FFFF **Evening meal** by request **Credit Cards** MC V **Children** yes **Disabled** no **Pets** yes **Closed** Jan, Feb **Languages** English **Proprietor** Charles-Henry de Valbray

St-Philbert-des-Champs, N of Lisieux

Ferme des Poiriers Roses

Flowers are everywhere in this thatched, half-timbered, 17thC Norman farmhouse: fresh, dried and in pot-pourris. All come from the owners' garden. The bedrooms, named after musical heroines such as Lara and Kalinka, are in the main house and in the converted stables. Even the bread at breakfast receives favourable reviews. In the garden are apple and pear trees plus an antique calvados distillery.

Directions 8 km N of Lisieux. D 579 to Ouilly; right on D 98 for St-Philbert. After 4 km, right on D 264. Farm on left, before village.

❖ 14130 St-Philbert-des-Champs **Tel** 31 64 72 14 **Fax** 31 64 19 55 **Rooms** 7 **Prices** FFF **Evening meal** no **Credit Cards** no **Children** yes **Disabled** no **Pets** no **Closed** never **Languages** English **Proprietors** Jacques and Elizabeth Lecorneur

St-Pierre-de-Plesg., SE of Dinan

Le Petit Moulin du Rouvre

The carefully renovated 17thC mill with its water-wheel is surrounded by apple trees, fields and sheep. Inside, tapestries, old plates and antique guns line the walls. Each bedroom is different: the Chambre Marine has blue-and-white striped fabric with paintings of boats. Even after 20 years, the owner still enjoys having guests; her prices are reasonable and her dinners delicious, especially *volaille farcie*. One of our favourites.

Directions 15 km SE of Dinan. Take D 794, turn left on D 78. Follow signs.

❖ 35720 St-Pierre-de-Plesguen **Tel** 99 73 85 84 **Fax** 99 73 71 06 **Rooms** 4 **Prices** FFF **Evening meal** by request **Credit Cards** no **Children** yes **Disabled** no **Pets** yes **Closed** never; telephone in winter **Languages** French only **Proprietor** Annie Michel-Québriac

Servon, SW of Avranches

Le Petit Manoir

In 1990, the owners decided to redecorate but ended up renovating their farmhouse and using two spare rooms for bed-and-breakfast. It is a working farm, with animal noises and smells. Annick makes yoghurts for breakfast and, in deference to British guests, often serves afternoon tea. An *auberge* just 300 m away serves dinner. Bedrooms and bathrooms are rustic but comfortable, with distant views of Mont-St-Michel.

Directions 14 km SW of Avranches. Take N 276, N 175. Servon is off on right. Follow signs.

❖ 50170 Servon **Tel** 33 60 03 44 **Rooms** 2 **Prices** FF **Evening meal** no **Credit Cards** no **Children** yes **Disabled** no **Pets** yes **Closed** never **Languages** English, German, Italian **Proprietor** Annick Gedouin-Lavarec

Sourdeval, S of Vire

La Maurandière

Once the children had left home, the owners wanted "to meet people and keep busy". The result is one of the most comfortable and welcoming homes we visited. The 18thC stone farmhouse has family treasures such as old pewter and an amazing grandfather clock. Bedrooms are romantic, with grandmother's wardrobe and spinning-wheel in one, beams and a view of the garden in another. A converted sheepfold is a third room. Delightful.

Directions 15 km S of Vire. Take D 977; go through Sourdeval; cross river; take D 499 on left. Follow signs. On D 182.

❖ 50150 Sourdeval **Tel** 33 59 65 44 **Rooms** 4 **Prices** FF
Evening meal no **Credit Cards** no **Children** yes **Disabled** no
Pets yes **Closed** never **Languages** French only
Proprietor Evelyne Dupart

Tonquédec, NW of Guingamp

Le Queffiou

We were impressed by the neatness: the enormous, well-mown lawn, the gladioli and rose beds, silver birches and pampas grass. Families are welcome, as the children's swing testifies. Pink stone from the nearby granite coast frames the windows with their peach-coloured curtains. The owner has a strong sense of design and has decorated bedrooms boldly in a mix of styles. She also offers well-prepared, if somewhat expensive, evening meals.

Directions 22 km NW of Guingamp. Take D 767. Left at Cavan. Continue on road to castle. Well-signposted.

❖ route du Château, 22140 Tonquédec **Tel** 96 35 84 50
Rooms 5 **Prices** FFF **Evening meal** by request **Credit Cards** no
Children yes **Disabled** no **Pets** no **Closed** mid-Sept to mid-Jan
Languages English **Proprietor** Mme Sadoc

Château de la Ville-Guérif

Some visitors are intimidated by this small stately home owned by the local mayor. Huge pine and ash trees surround the lawn and steep stone steps lead to the entrance, with a magnificent staircase inside the front door. A grand piano, antiques and portraits of the viscount's ancestors sustain the impressive effect. Bedrooms and bathrooms are colour co-ordinated and although showing signs of wear and tear, still make a stylish base for a seaside holiday.

Directions 16 km SW of Dinard. Take D 168, D 786. At Trégon, turn right for Bay of Beaussais. Signposted.

❖ 22650 Trégon **Tel** 96 27 24 93 **Rooms** 5 **Prices** FFF
Evening meal no **Credit Cards** no **Children** yes **Disabled** no
Pets no **Closed** Oct to May **Languages** English, German
Proprietor Vicomte Stanislas de Pontbriand

La Ferme du Breil

Although the two-storey farmhouse is by a noisy roundabout, bedrooms face inwards, so are quiet. Everything from the buildings to the garden is well-maintained by the enthusiastic owner. The smell of breakfast is equally attractive: local breads served in the guests' sitting-room, with leather chairs. The bedrooms have beamed ceilings, elegant but not sumptuous furniture and blue bathrooms. Popular with guests from all over the world.

Directions 14 km SW of Dinard. Take D 168, D 786. House on left at intersection with D 26.

❖ 22650 Trégon **Tel** 96 27 30 55 **Rooms** 4 **Prices** FF
Evening meal no **Credit Cards** no **Children** yes **Disabled** no
Pets yes **Closed** never **Languages** English **Proprietor** Comtesse de Blacas

Trégrom, W of Guingamp

Le Presbytère

With walled gardens, roses, apple trees, lawns and a swing, this L-shaped former rectory has a fairy tale effect according to one visitor. A scent of wood smoke hangs in the beautifully decorated rooms full of books. The church is visible through the small bedroom windows. The owner, who used to run a château-hotel, serves outstanding meals in her yellow-and-blue kitchen/dining room: salmon *en papillotte*, smoked trout, apple tart.

Directions 20 km W of Guingamp. Take N 12 to Belle-Isle exit. Go N on D 33. Across from church in village.

❖ Trégrom, 22420 Plouaret **Tel** 96 47 94 15 **Rooms** 3 **Prices** FF **Evening meal** by request **Credit Cards** no **Children** yes **Disabled** no **Pets** yes **Closed** never **Languages** English **Proprietor** Nicole de Morchoven

La Trinité-sur-Mer, S of Auray

La Maison du Latz

A delightful combination of position and personality. The house is plain and white but it sits right on the water. The wrap-around glassed-in terrace, like the bedrooms, looks south over the river estuary and sailing boats. One bedroom has a brass bedstead, hand-crocheted bedspread and floral curtains. Bathrooms are modern and white. Dinners of seafood, fish and home-made desserts are well-priced. Convivial ambience, lively, helpful owner.

Directions 15 km S of Auray. Take D 28 to Pont de Kerisper. Cross bridge and turn right to Le Latz. At water's edge.

❖ Le Latz, 56470 La Trinité-sur-Mer **Tel** 97 55 80 91 **Rooms** 4 **Prices** FF **Evening meal** by request **Credit Cards** no **Children** yes **Disabled** no **Pets** no **Closed** never **Languages** English **Proprietor** Nicole Le Rouzic

La Turballe, NW of La Baule

Les Rochasses

Those planning a family holiday near the sea may find the Elains' comfortable but plain, modern home useful. It is at the back of La Turballe, a fishing port but "you can only just see the sea," admits Colette, the cheerful owner, who has two bedrooms in her house and three more in the *pavillon* by the 10 m by 5 m swimming-pool (with diving-board). Furniture is contemporary; bathrooms are small but towels are thick.

Directions 12 km NW of La Baule. Take D 99. Rue de Bellevue is on left between bvd de Lauvergnac and port. House on left.

❖ 58 rue de Bellevue, 44420 La Turballe **Tel** 40 23 31 29
Rooms 5 **Prices** FF **Evening meal** no **Credit Cards** no
Children yes **Disabled** no **Pets** yes **Closed** never
Languages French only **Proprietors** Michel and Colette Elain

Verrières, NW of Nogent-le-Rotrou

La Berdrie

A stylish country hideaway. Rooms are light and not overly furnished, so the few handsome pieces of antique furniture stand out. Breakfast is in a huge salon with open fireplace, plants, oriental fabrics and rattan furniture. Bedrooms are up a steep staircase: one is split-level, the bed tucked under beams; the other is 'sumptuous', with red and gold wallpaper and matching 1930s bed, table and chairs. The shared bathroom is attractive.

Directions 10 km NW of Nogent-le-Rotrou. Take D 955; right on D 11. Signposted on left, 2 km after Dancé.

❖ Verrières, 61110 Rémalard **Tel** 33 73 84 73 **Rooms** 2
Prices FF **Evening meal** by request **Credit Cards** no
Children yes **Disabled** no **Pets** no **Closed** mid-Dec to 1 Jan
Languages French only **Proprietors** M and Mme Raquois

➤ *More on page 161*

Milly-la-Forêt, S of Paris

Ferme de la Grange Rouge

Although this is a working farm, growing cereals and sugar beet, there are no longer any animals so the family converted a huge stone barn into bedrooms. Colour schemes are bright and modern, offsetting the old beams and rustic look. Breakfast is in the barn's sitting-room/dining-room; guests go 3 km to Milly-la-Forêt for dinner. Useful for overnights and seeing Fontainebleau.
Directions 65 km S of Paris. Take A 6; then exit 11 Auvernaux. Take D 948 via Milly-la-Forêt, then D 837, D 449 for Gironville. Signposted 'La Grange Rouge'.

❖ 91490 Milly-la-Forêt **Tel** 1 64 98 94 21 **Fax** 1 64 98 99 91
Rooms 5 **Prices** FF **Evening meal** no **Credit Cards** no
Children yes **Disabled** no **Pets** no **Closed** never
Languages English **Proprietors** Sophie and Charles Desforges

Pommeuse, E of Paris

Cottage du Martin Pécheur

"We opened at the same time as Euro Disney," laughs Annie, whose husband renovated their charming, 19thC stone home in 1992, named after the kingfishers that flit along the Grand Morin river in summer. The garden runs down to the stream. Her daughters married Englishmen, she likes English china and linens, but breakfasts are French. Her guests are so keen on her jams that she often runs out – indeed she gives jars away as gifts.
Directions 60 km E of Paris. Take A 4; exit Crécy-la-Chapelle. Take N 34 for Coulommiers. Village on right. House by river.

❖ 1 rue des Iris, 77515 Pommeuse **Tel** 1 64 20 00 98
Fax 1 64 20 03 06 **Rooms** 4 **Prices** FF **Evening meal** no
Credit Cards no **Children** yes **Disabled** no **Pets** no **Closed** never
Languages English **Proprietors** Jacky and Annie Thomas

Thoiry-en-Yvelines, W of Paris

Château de Thoiry

The Panouse family exploit this 400-year-old mansion to pay for its upkeep: 800 animals in a wildlife park, film crews making movies in the gilded *salons*. Guests can pretend to live like a lord, including breakfast in bed served by a butler. Combined with one of Thoiry's special events like a concert, this is pure theatrical extravagance. One bedroom has 18thC furniture; the duplex apartment has two working Louis XV fireplaces.

Directions From Paris, go W on the A 13. Exit at Bois d'Arcy, for Dreux. At Pontchartrain, take the D 11 to Thoiry.

❖ 78770 Thoiry-en-Yvelines **Tel** 34 87 52 25 **Fax** 34 87 54 12
Rooms 4 **Prices** FFFF **Evening meal** by request **Credit Cards** MC V **Children** yes **Disabled** no **Pets** yes **Closed** never
Languages English **Proprietors** Vicomte and Vicomtesse de la Panouse

Thomery, E of Fontainebleau

Vivescence

Creeper-covered, with neat lawns and flower-beds, this attractive town house has been converted into a health spa by a qualified physiotherapist. The ambience may be somewhat antiseptic, especially in the wing where seminars are held, but the sauna and heated indoor swimming-pool compensate. Bicycle in the local lanes. Eat in the house or try restaurants in the pretty village. Trains to Gare de Lyon, Paris from local station (45 mins).

Directions 7 km E of Fontainebleau. Take N 6; turn left on D 301. House is opposite church.

❖ 9 place Greffuhle, 77810 Thomery **Tel** 1 60 96 43 96
Fax 1 60 96 41 13 **Rooms** 6 **Prices** FFF **Evening meal** by request **Credit Cards** MC V **Children** no **Disabled** no **Pets** no
Closed last week Dec **Languages** English
Proprietor Brigitte Stacke

➡ *More on page 161*

Ancemont, S of Verdun

Château de la Bessière

Close to Verdun and First World War monuments, the Eichenauers have restored this graceful 18thC château on a small side street. Rooms are spacious and airy with tastefully chosen furniture. There is a coat of arms at the back of the grate in the stone fireplace in the reception hall. Bedrooms are lavishly, even romantically, decorated in the *belle époque* style, with chandeliers and floral wallpaper. The swimming-pool was added in 1994.

Directions 10km S of Verdun. Take D 34 to Ancemont; rue du Four is a quiet side street.

❖ rue du Four, 55320 Ancemont **Tel** 29 85 70 21
Fax 29 87 61 60 **Rooms** 4 **Prices** FF **Evening meal** by request
Credit Cards no **Children** yes **Disabled** yes **Pets** yes
Closed never **Languages** English, German, Italian
Proprietors René and Marie-José Eichenauer

Arry-sur-Moselle, S of Metz

5 Grand'Rue

Arry is a pleasant spot on a hill above the Moselle River. The Finance family is known for its welcome, especially the generous 'eat as much as you want' dinner using home-grown produce. Undistinguished outside, with green shutters and window boxes; inside are rustic wood panelling and cosy bedrooms. The biggest sleeps two adults and four children; the prettiest has blue wallpaper. River views from top two floors. Small courtyard.

Directions 18 km S of Metz. Take N 57. Arry-sur-Moselle on left above river. House is on main street.

❖ 5 Grand'Rue, 57680 Arry-sur-Moselle **Tel** 87 52 83 95
Rooms 5 **Prices** FF **Evening meal** by request **Credit Cards** AE
DC MC V **Children** yes **Disabled** no **Pets** yes **Closed** never
Languages English, German, Italian **Proprietor** Nadia Finance

---

Breuschwickersheim, W of Strasb.

La Ferme Martzloff

The Diemer family has lived in this rambling farmhouse since 1792. The oldest parts of the half-timbered building are medieval; in comparison the modern bedrooms somewhat soulless. All look south over the garden: two are spacious, but even the four under the eaves are large. It is the Diemers themselves that make this popular year round. If they are full, their cousins nearby take the overspill. Swimming-pool.

Directions 12 km W of Strasbourg. Take D 45. On main street; look for signs.

❖ 51 rue Principale, 67112 Breuschwickersheim
Tel 88 96 02 89 **Rooms** 6 **Prices** FF **Evening meal** no
Credit Cards MC V **Children** yes **Disabled** no **Pets** no
Closed never **Languages** German **Proprietors** Eliane and Alfred Diemer

Cirey-sur-Vezouze, E of Blâmont

18 rue du Val

'A family environment with no frills,' was the verdict on this house on the edge of town. Rooms are big: a marble bust surveys the sitting-room; there is also a billiard room. Bedrooms are equally spacious but simply furnished; bathrooms were modernised recently. Monique Bouvery's Alsace and Lorraine dishes feature in a well-priced evening meal. With a large garden and garages, it is a useful base for touring the Vosges Mountains.

Directions 9 km E of Blâmont. Take D 993 to Cirey. Follow signs in town.

❖ 18 rue du Val, 54480 Cirey-sur-Vezouze **Tel** 83 42 58 38
Rooms 5 **Prices** FF **Evening meal** by request **Credit Cards** no
Children yes **Disabled** no **Pets** yes **Closed** never
Languages some English **Proprietors** Daniel and Monique Bouvery

Cosswiller-W., W of Strasbourg

Le Tirelire

On a single track road near the enchanting village, the turn-of-the-century villa looks more German than French. The dignified, friendly owner has prettily decorated bedrooms with Laura Ashley wallpaper. One has a canopied bed with blue curtains and a Chinese carpet; another, a pink gingham bedspread and pink curtains. Views are of the large garden or the Vosges Mountains. On the Wine Road, cellars nearby: an inn next door for dinner.

Directions 28 km W of Strasbourg. Take N 4 to Wasselonne; D 22 left to Cosswiller. Follow signs in village.

❖ 2 Hameau Tirelire, 67310 Coswiller **Tel** 88 87 22 49
Rooms 5 **Prices** FFF **Evening meal** no **Credit Cards** no
Children yes **Disabled** yes **Pets** no **Closed** Jan; mid-June to mid-July **Languages** some English, Italian **Proprietor** Madame Maud Bochart

Cuvry, S of Metz

Ferme de Haute-Rive

Nothing can be heard but songbirds and dogs barking at this small farm on a country road. Built on the remains of a 12thC military tower, a vine climbs along the ancient walls. Although the interior has beamed ceilings and some bedrooms have solid mahogany bedsteads, all the bathrooms are modern, renewed in 1990 when the Morhains first took guests. Hearty local dishes are served using farm produce. Pleasant garden.

Directions 10 km S of Metz. Take D 5. Turn left for Cuvry; follow signs.

❖ 57420 Cuvry **Tel** 87 52 50 08 **Fax** 87 52 60 20 **Rooms** 4
Prices FF **Evening meal** by request **Credit Cards** no
Children yes **Disabled** no **Pets** no **Closed** Dec to Feb
Languages English, German **Proprietors** Brigitte and Jean-François Morhain

Dieffenbach-au-Val, NW of Sélestat

La Romance

This was one of the best places visited by our inspectors in the region. Built in 1992 in traditional style and specifically to take guests, bedrooms are named after their colour schemes: Lavender, Cornflower Blue. All have fitted cupboards, some have state-of-the-art bathrooms. The attic bedroom is romantic. Views are of wooded hillsides or the valley; there are swings in the garden and wine cellars nearby to visit. Minimum two night stay.
Directions 12 km NW of Sélestat on D 424. Just before Thanvillé, turn left on D 697 to Dieffenbach. Follow signs in village.

❖ 17 route de Neuve-Eglise, 67220 Dieffenbach-au-Val
Tel 88 85 67 09 **Fax** 88 85 69 76 **Rooms** 4 **Prices** FF
Evening meal no **Credit Cards** no **Children** yes **Disabled** no
Pets no **Closed** never **Languages** German, some English
Proprietors Serge and Corinne Geiger

Rezonville, W of Metz

2 Hameau de Flavigny

Although this is a plain building, the Lambinets make it attractive with white shutters and a terrace brightened by tubs of geraniums. An old cartwheel leans against an acacia tree. With table tennis, mountain bikes and a children's slide in the paddock, this is popular with families. Betty's cooking is praised for local Lorraine dishes, fruit tarts and sorbets. Bedrooms are comfortable. There is an old baker's oven in the sitting-room.
Directions 20 km W of Metz . Take D 903 to Rezonville. Turn left 3 km beyond Rezonville to Flavigny. Follow signs.

❖ 57130 Rezonville **Tel** 87 31 40 13 **Rooms** 3 **Prices** FF
Evening meal by request **Credit Cards** MC V **Children** yes
Disabled no **Pets** no **Closed** Nov to March **Languages** English,
German **Proprietors** Elisabeth and Francis Lambinet

➡ *More on page 170*

Ardenais, E of la Châtre

Domaine de Vilotte

Although the Champeniers visit at weekends, their housekeepers look after guests in this handsome, rose-covered mansion. The family feeling, however, remains thanks to their collection of antique radios, telephones and sewing machines that fills the entrance, and the old plates that brighten the dining-room. The farmhouse-style kitchen is lined with copper pans and the elegant bedrooms are decorated with family paintings and photos.
Directions 33 km E of la Châtre. D 940 N for Bourges. Right at Thevet-St-Julien on D 951 for Vilotte, just beyond Le Châtelet.

❖ Ardenais, 18170 Le Châtelet-en-Berry
Tel and Fax 48 96 04 96 **Rooms** 5 **Prices** FFF **Evening meal** by request **Credit Cards** no **Children** yes **Disabled** no **Pets** yes **Closed** Oct to March **Languages** English **Proprietors** Jacques and Yolande Champenier

Azay-le-Rideau

Le Clos Philippa

Next to one of the prettiest châteaux in France. Unimpressive outside, the late-18thC house is attractive within. A collection of old straw hats brightens the hall. Rooms are large, with high ceilings, antiques. Up a spiral staircase, bedrooms have views of the château across the elegant garden. Bathrooms are small but clean. Breakfast is in the impressive dining-room. An ideal base for exploring the region. Charming hostess. Secure parking.
Directions Next to the château on the E side of the town.

❖ 10 rue Pineau, 37190 Azay-le-Rideau **Tel** 47 45 26 49
Rooms 4 **Prices** FF **Evening meal** no **Credit Cards** V **Children** yes **Disabled** no **Pets** yes **Closed** never; telephone in winter **Languages** French only **Proprietor** Bernadette Wilmann

Azay-le-Rideau

La Petite Loge

On a large estate with horses and vineyards on the outskirts of Azay-le-Rideau, the owner has well-priced, plain bedrooms that are popular with walkers and tourists. Four are up a wooden staircase in the main house, one is on the ground floor: all are clean and comfortable. Guests are welcome to use the kitchen next to the dining-room to prepare evening meals, picnics or food to barbecue in the grounds. Restaurants 1 km in village.

Directions 1 km N of Azay-le-Rideau. Take D 751. Look for signs on left.

❖ 15 route de Tours, 37190 Azay-le-Rideau **Tel** 47 45 26 05
Fax 47 45 33 21 **Rooms** 5 **Prices** FF **Evening meal** no
Credit Cards no **Children** yes **Disabled** no **Pets** no
Closed never; telephone in winter **Languages** English
Proprietor Thierry Poireau

Azay-sur-Cher, E of Tours

Château du Coteau

A grand piano is a reminder that Chopin was a regular visitor. It is easy to see why: peacocks strut in the vast park, a caged song-bird greets guests at the entrance. The attractively decorated bedrooms are in the Clock House, a separate building. One has peach walls, a green carpet plus matching curtains and bedspread. The apartment, with a double bed and three singles, also has a kitchen. High quality but reasonable prices.

Directions 15 km E of Tours. Take N 76 up Cher Valley. 1 km after Azay on left. Signposted.

❖ 37270 Azay-sur-Cher **Tel** 47 50 47 47 **Fax** 47 50 49 60
Rooms 6 **Prices** FFF **Evening meal** no **Credit Cards** MC V
Children yes **Disabled** no **Pets** yes **Closed** never
Languages English, Italian **Proprietor** Pierre-Claude Tassi

Azay-sur-Cher, SE of Tours

Le Patouillard

A working farm 'with smells to match' reported our inspectors after a comfortable night here. Dinner was substantial and high-lighted by liberal quantities of the owner's father's red wine. The hosts are friendly enough but have small children, so are not able to spend much time with guests. Bedrooms and the combined sitting-room/dining-room, separate from the main house, are plain, clean and modern. Convenient, attractively priced.

Directions 10 km SE of Tours. Take N 76 through Azay-sur-Cher. Look for signs on right.

❖ 37270 Azay-sur-Cher **Tel** 47 50 41 32 **Fax** 47 50 47 65 **Rooms** 3 **Prices** FF **Evening meal** by request **Credit Cards** no **Children** yes **Disabled** no **Pets** yes **Closed** never; telephone in winter **Languages** some English **Proprietors** M and Mme Moreau

Azé, NW of Vendôme

Ferme de Crislaine

The owners have modernised their ivy-clad red-brick farmhouse, leaving some beams and bricks exposed under high, wood-lined ceilings. With a separate entrance to the bedrooms, long-stay guests have privacy plus the use of a kitchen, though the low price and admirable quality of evening meals make this facility redundant. Toys, swings, table tennis, bicycles and a swimming-pool keep children happy. An above-average base for the Loire Valley.

Directions 9 km NW of Vendôme. Take D 957, D 24 to Azé. Clearly signposted.

❖ Azé, 41100 Vendôme **Tel** 54 72 14 09 **Rooms** 5 **Prices** FF **Evening meal** by request **Credit Cards** no **Children** yes **Disabled** no **Pets** yes **Closed** never; telephone in winter **Languages** English, German, Spanish **Proprietors** Christian and Annie Guellier

Azé, NW of Vendôme

Ferme des Gourmets

The modern bedrooms at this working farm are nothing special, 'just clean and comfortable', but there is plenty to do: a tennis court, table tennis, bicycles and an arrangement for swimming at the nearby Ferme de Crislaine (see page 77). Meals are above average: breakfast with cereals, yoghurt; dinner with farm produce. There is also the owner's sister's *ferme auberge* two minutes away. Their speciality shop sells a wide range of organic gourmet foods.

Directions 9 km NW of Vendôme. Take D 957. Farm signposted on right before Azé turn-off.

❖ Azé, 41100 Vendôme **Tel** 54 72 04 16 **Rooms** 6 **Prices** FF
Evening meal by request **Credit Cards** no **Children** yes
Disabled no **Pets** yes **Closed** never; telephone in winter
Languages English **Proprietors** Michel and Nadége Boulai

Blaison, SE of Angers

Château de Cheman

The elderly owner is known for her award-winning wines, so bed-and-breakfast is secondary. The ancient limestone building looks in need of some repair. Inside are echoing rooms, stone floors, large lumpy furniture and crossed swords on the walls. Up spiral stairs, in a tower, the bedrooms are more pleasant: two have TV, terrace, sitting-room and kitchenette. Well-sited in the Loire Valley, but expensive and somewhat impersonal.

Directions 20 km SE of Angers. Take N 260, D 748 to Brissac-Quincé. Then left on D 55 for Blaison. Just before village.

❖ Blaison, 49320 Brissac-Quincé **Tel** 41 57 17 60 **Rooms** 3
Prices FFFF **Evening meal** no **Credit Cards** no **Children** yes
Disabled no **Pets** no **Closed** never; telephone ahead
Languages French only **Proprietor** Mme Alvina Antoine

Bourges

Bonnets Rouges

We wish there were more bed-and-breakfasts in cities. Marie-Ange Brouste converted her 16thC house into a rather bohemian *maison d'hôtes*. Set in a courtyard, with dormer windows and a walled garden, it is in the medieval heart of Bourges, just off the historic rue Bourbonnoux. Bedrooms are themed: one is Empire style, another is 1950s, a third is rustic. Many choose the more cramped *romantique* under the ancient roof. Distinctly different.

Directions rue de la Thaumassière is off the pedestrianised Rue Bourbonnoux not far from the cathedral.

❖ 3 rue de la Thaumassière, 18000 Bourges **Tel** 48 65 79 92
Fax 48 69 82 05 **Rooms** 4 **Prices** FFF **Evening meal** no
Credit Cards no **Children** yes **Disabled** no **Pets** no **Closed** never
Languages some English **Proprietor** Marie-Ange Brouste

Champigné, N of Angers

Château des Briottières

François and his Danish wife have five children who take the formality out of this vast, 18thC country mansion where the film *L'Impromptu* was shot. One of the first *châteaux* to offer bed-and-breakfast, this couple have the right formula, ensuring that guests are not overawed by bathrooms that are more like *salons* than *salles de bains*. Children can play in the heated swimming-pool in the old kitchen garden.

Directions 25 km N of Angers. Take N 162; at Lion d'Angers turn E on D 770. Take D 768, then D 190.

❖ 49330 Champigné **Tel** 41 42 00 02 **Fax** 41 42 01 55 **Rooms** 10
Prices FFFF **Evening meal** by request **Credit Cards** AE DC MC V
Children yes **Disabled** no **Pets** yes **Closed** never
Languages English, Spanish **Proprietors** François and Hedwige de Valbray

Charenton-Laugère, E of St-Amand

La Serre

Despite its Norman-looking, brown and cream half-timbering, this manor house was actually built in the 1940s. The owner is a painter who collects and restores art deco furniture, and the house is full of paintings and sculptures by young artists of today. All the bedrooms are vast and overlook secluded formal gardens. The cooking is done by both husband and wife. There is only one complication: both husband and wife are called Claude.

Directions 15 km E of St-Amand-Montrond. Take D 951. From Charenton-Laugère, D 953 to Dun. Manor house 400 m on left.

❖ Route de Dun, 18210 Charenton-Laugère **Tel** 48 60 75 82
Rooms 3 **Prices** FFF **Evening meal** by request **Credit Cards** V
Children yes **Disabled** no **Pets** yes **Closed** never
Languages English **Proprietors** Claude and Claude Moreau

Chauvigny, E of Poitiers

8 rue du Berry

Right in the middle of town, the secluded back garden of this 18thC home has trees, roses and a fine view of the ruined castle. Opened for bed-and-breakfast in 1992, the family atmosphere persists thanks to the heirlooms throughout. A piano stands in the hall; there is central heating. One bedroom has been adapted for disabled access. Evening meals are a bargain and cars are locked behind gates at night. Value for money, genuine welcome.

Directions 18 km E of Poitiers. Take N 151. In middle of town, near the Town Hall, Notre-Dame church, off rue du Marché.

❖ 8 rue du Berry, 86300 Chauvigny **Tel** 49 46 30 81
Fax 49 47 64 12 **Rooms** 6 **Prices** FF **Evening meal** by request
Credit Cards no **Children** yes **Disabled** yes **Pets** no **Closed** Nov
to March **Languages** English **Proprietors** Jacques and Claude de
Giafferri

Cravant-les-Côteaux, E of Chinon

Pallus

Antiques are everywhere – the owner is an expert. His home and small shop are in the Vienne vineyards. A display of fob watches and glass sculptures caught our eye. All bedrooms are spacious with beautiful white bed-linens, embroidered with the owner's initials on the pillowcases. Outside, a walled garden hides a swimming-pool. Breakfast is eaten outdoors as often as possible. An ideal base for exploring the Loire valley.

Directions 10 km E of Chinon. Take D 21; house on right beyond Cravant-les-Côteaux.

❖ 37500 Cravant-les-Côteaux **Tel** 47 93 08 94 **Fax** 47 98 43 00 **Rooms** 3 **Prices** FFF **Evening meal** no **Credit Cards** no **Children** no **Disabled** no **Pets** no **Closed** never; telephone **Languages** English, German **Proprietors** Bernard and Barbara Chauveau

Doix, S of Fontenay-le-Comte

Le Logis de Chalusseau

There is a medieval but comfortable ambience in the beamed bedrooms at the Baudry family's 17thC home in the marshes. One has a painted stone fireplace with a blue-curtained canopy bed. Breakfast is in the old dining-room, but guests are welcome to use the refrigerator to prepare themselves an evening meal, although there are restaurants nearby. Marie-Thérèse is helpful and hospitable so this is a good base to explore the region.

Directions 9 km S of Fontenay-le-Comte. D 938 for La Rochelle; left on D 68 through Ecoué, Doux. Sign on right before Doix.

❖ Chalusseau, 85200 Doix **Tel** 51 51 81 12 **Rooms** 3 **Prices** FF **Evening meal** no **Credit Cards** no **Children** yes **Disabled** no **Pets** no **Closed** never; telephone in winter **Languages** English **Proprietors** Gérard and Marie-Thérèse Baudry

Les Essards, NW of Saintes

Le Pinier

Jean-Claude Jamin is a real farmer with animals, maize and a lively *basse-cour* (farmyard), which children enjoy. Two plain bedrooms are in the main house, three more in a converted outbuilding with a sitting-room. All the bathrooms are modern. Evening meals are a bargain, with farm vegetables and meat or perhaps *mouclade* (a local mussel dish). The beach is a half-hour drive away, bicycle and walking trails cross the farm. Well-priced.

Directions 10 km NW of Saintes. Take N 137; left on D 119 to Les Essards; left on D 237 towards St-Georges. Signposted.

❖ 17250 Les Essards **Tel** 46 93 91 43 **Fax** 46 93 93 64 **Rooms** 5 **Prices** FF **Evening meal** by request **Credit Cards** no **Children** yes **Disabled** no **Pets** yes **Closed** never **Languages** English **Proprietor** Jean-Claude Jamin

Esvres, E of Montbazon

Château de Vaugrignon

It needs an abrupt turn to get through the imposing gateway and up the steep driveway to find this elegant 15thC mansion high above the Indre River. At the gatehouse is the owner's thriving antiques business. Through the arch are converted stables with five attractive bedrooms: fresh, modern, with some beams exposed and one or two antiques such as a wardrobe. Guests may sit on the gravelled terrace overlooking a formal garden.

Directions 6 km E of Montbazon. Take D 17. Château on left before Esvres.

❖ 37320 Esvres **Tel** 47 26 29 86 **Rooms** 5 **Prices** FF **Evening meal** no **Credit Cards** no **Children** yes **Disabled** no **Pets** no **Closed** never **Languages** English **Proprietor** Emmanuel Barthélemy

Farges-Allichamps, NW of St-Amand

Château de la Commanderie

'Expensive but worth every penny, the sort of place you would pay to look 'round,' reported one guest. The atmosphere is of 100 years ago but everything has been well-maintained, from the furnishings to the park, with its horses bred for steeplechasing. Bedrooms are elegant: exotic birds on curtains and bedcovers feature in one, whose bathroom is in a turret. Family portraits in the drawing-room observe guests meeting for pre-dinner drinks.
Directions 12 km NW of St-Amand-Montrond. N 144 to Bruère-Allichamps; D 92 over river, A 71. Signs in Farges-Allichamps.

❖ 18200 St-Amand-Montrond **Tel** 48 61 04 19 **Fax** 48 61 01 84
Rooms 8 **Prices** FFFF **Evening meal** by request **Credit Cards** MC
V **Children** yes **Disabled** no **Pets** yes **Closed** never
Languages English **Proprietors** Comte and Comtesse de
Jouffroy-Gonsans

Foécy, NW of Bourges

Le Petit Prieuré

Tall wooden gates protect the privacy of this cottage in a quiet village. The owner, a sculptor who lectures on fine arts, has his works everywhere in the house which has a terrace and garden. The friendly host likes to give a personal, if somewhat eccentric, touch to everything from bathrooms to the breakfast: a plastic flower by the wash-basin, a real flower by the butter. We prefer the small but recently decorated bedrooms above his studio.
Directions 25 km NW of Bourges. Take N 76 via Mehun for Vierzon; before Vignoux, turn left on D 30. House is near church.

❖ 7 rue de l'Eglise, 18500 Foécy **Tel** 48 51 01 76 **Rooms** 3
Prices FF **Evening meal** no **Credit Cards** no **Children** yes
Disabled no **Pets** no **Closed** never **Languages** English, Italian
Proprietor Claude Alard

Grez-Neuville, NW of Angers

La Croix d'Etain

An elegant country house in a delightful setting: lawns run down to the Mayenne River in a small village where boats may be hired. Bedrooms are large, luxurious and well-decorated with a floral theme throughout. There are magazines plus tea and coffee-making facilities. Furniture is antique but bathrooms are modern with fluffy towels. The owners, a retired couple, prepare an elaborate evening meal, with fresh river fish in season.

Directions 20 km NW of Angers. Take N 162, right on D 291 to village. At the church, follow rue de l'Ecluse to the riverbank.

❖ 2 rue de l'Ecluse, 49220 Grez-Neuville **Tel** 41 95 68 49 **Rooms** 4 **Prices** FFF **Evening meal** by request **Credit Cards** no **Children** yes **Disabled** no **Pets** yes **Closed** never; telephone in winter **Languages** English, some German **Proprietors** Jacqueline and Auguste Bahuaud

Ingrandes de Touraine, E of Bourgueil

Le Clos St-André

The owners enjoy talking about wine and antiques over dinner which might include leek tart, wood pigeon with mushrooms, salad, cheese and *crème caramel*. Their 16thC house is slowly being refurbished rather than modernized, so original features such as wood floors and beams survive. A separate entrance and a stone staircase lead to the surprisingly large bedrooms, with firm beds. An outstanding base in the Loire valley.

Directions 7 km E of Bourgueil. Take D 35. Clearly indicated in the middle of the village.

❖ Ingrandes de Touraine, 37140 Bourgueil **Tel** 47 96 90 81 **Rooms** 6 **Prices** FF **Evening meal** by request **Credit Cards** MC V **Children** yes **Disabled** no **Pets** yes **Closed** Christmas, 1 week Feb **Languages** English **Proprietors** M and Mme Pinçon

W of Le Lion d'Angers

Le Petit Carqueron

The cooking is the chief appeal at this 200-year-old farmhouse, renovated in the late 1980s. Home-made pâté, rabbit dishes, local cheeses, *clafoutis* and chocolate cake are praised by guests who dine by candlelight at a long antique table (outdoors in summer). By contrast, bedrooms are clean and modern but have inexpensive furniture. Showers are small and two bedrooms share a WC. It helps to be a dog-lover here. Value for money.

Directions 3 km W of Le Lion d'Angers. Take D 770. After 1.5 km turn left. House is signposted on right.

❖ 49220 Le Lion d'Angers **Tel** 41 95 62 65 **Rooms** 4 **Prices** FF
Evening meal by request **Credit Cards** no **Children** yes
Disabled no **Pets** no **Closed** Nov to Easter **Languages** English
Proprietors M and Mme Carcaillet

Luynes

Moulin Hodoux

After several years in West Africa, the owners returned to transform this old mill. A garden, stream and waterfall are at the back. The bedrooms have light, bright walls with a tasteful mixture of antique and 'modern' furniture: one has African souvenirs. Bathrooms are modern. The hostess enjoys cooking regional dishes from local produce and using the barbecue. Meals are taken on the sheltered porch. The swimming-pool is large.

Directions 1 km NW of Luynes. Take D 76 W from Luynes. Right on D 126 towards Vieux Bourg. Signposted.

❖ 37230 Luynes **Tel** 47 55 76 27 **Rooms** 4 **Prices** FFF
Evening meal by request **Credit Cards** no **Children** yes
Disabled no **Pets** yes **Closed** never **Languages** English, German
Proprietor Jocelyne Vacher

Le Quart

Deep in the country on a sheep-farming estate, this is 'like something out of the soap-opera *Dallas*,' with its avenue, courtyard and stables. Mme Descorps is English and loves detail: iced water in bedrooms, sheets changed daily, cars parked out of sight in the barn. Everything is top quality: American showers, mattresses, antiques, Laura Ashley fabrics, even Hermès porcelain at the breakfast-table. The drawback? No evening meal is served.
Directions 6 km N of Luynes. Take D 6 towards Pernay. Signposted Le Quart, on right.

❖ 37230 Luynes **Tel** 47 55 51 70 **Fax** 47 55 57 49 **Rooms** 4 **Prices** FFFF **Evening meal** no **Credit Cards** no **Children** yes **Disabled** yes **Pets** yes **Closed** never **Languages** English; some German, Italian, Spanish **Proprietors** M and Mme Michel Descorps

Marans

Barbecane

The 25-year-old house is on a quiet lane by the Sèvre River. The owner returned from South Africa in 1990. Bedrooms are carpeted, with central heating and individual colour schemes. The half-tiled bathrooms have first-class fittings. Guests are free to use the refrigerator, washing machine and barbecue. Swimming-pool, table-tennis and badminton are in the secluded garden. The house speciality is *mouclade*, with local mussels.
Directions on NE edge of Marans. Take rue d'Aligre, turn right after second bridge, drive along riverbank. Signposted on left.

❖ Rive Droite de la Sèvre, 17230 Marans **Tel** 46 01 02 71 **Fax** 46 01 16 77 **Rooms** 6 **Prices** FFF **Evening meal** by request **Credit Cards** no **Children** yes **Disabled** yes **Pets** yes **Closed** Oct to Feb **Languages** English **Proprietor** Mr G Wilde

Mareuil, NE of Cognac

Les Hiboux

A fine example of a Charente farm complex with courtyard, oak beams and stone walls preserved by the British owners who put antiques in the sitting-room, Victorian pieces in the bedrooms. Two are 'de luxe', three are cheaper with simpler bathrooms. Full in July and August, off-season is enjoyable with wine appreciation courses. Jean's cooking is praised for French and 'international' dishes, often using abundant local seafood.

Directions 15 km NE of Cognac. Take D 15 to Sigogne; bear left on D 75; left again on D 119. House on left.

❖ La Courade, 16170 Mareuil **Tel** 45 96 51 55 **Fax** 45 96 52 53 **Rooms** 6 **Prices** FFF-FFFF **Evening meal** yes **Credit Cards** no **Children** yes **Disabled** no **Pets** no **Closed** never **Languages** English, German, Italian, Spanish, Portuguese **Proprietors** Richard and Jean Strickland

Mervent, NE of Fontenay-le-Comte

Logis de la Cornelière

Some guests stay here just to pick mushrooms in the surrounding woods. Built of mustard-coloured stone, the atmospheric, squat house retains its 17thC character: spacious rooms have antique furniture and carved stone fireplaces. Those who want to relax and sleep late may opt for brunch instead of breakfast. Expensive, since there is no evening meal. Set deep in the Vendée's vast Mervent-Vouvant national forest. Restaurant 4 km.

Directions 13 km NE of Fontenay-le-Comte. Take D 938. Turn right on D 99. House is 4 km beyond Mervent on right.

❖ 85200 Mervent **Tel** 51 00 29 25 **Rooms** 2 **Prices** FFFF **Evening meal** no **Credit Cards** no **Children** yes **Disabled** yes **Pets** yes **Closed** never **Languages** English **Proprietors** Jean-Raymond and Lyse de Larocque Latour

Mettray, NW of Tours

Moulin Neuf

A 17thC mill on the Choisille River with a park, walled swimming-pool, tennis-court and a beat for fishing. The mill stream runs under a glass floor in the garden-room. Rugs cover stone floors, and bedrooms are larger than usual with television and an elegant mixture of antique and modern furniture beneath beamed ceilings. The bathrooms, with large fluffy towels, are also modern. The owner has a collection of toy elephants.

Directions 4 km NW of Tours. Take N 138, then D 76 to Mettray. Signpost on gate.

❖ 33 rue du Vieux Calvaire, 37390 Mettray **Tel** 47 54 47 62
Fax 47 41 53 37 **Rooms** 4 **Prices** FFF **Evening meal** no
Credit Cards no **Children** yes **Disabled** no **Pets** no
Closed never; telephone in winter **Languages** some English
Proprietor Annick Samuzeau

Montigny, SW of Sancerre

La Reculée

Across from the main house, in the former stables of a classic four-sided farm, are a sitting-room with a fireplace plus five attractive bedrooms named for flowers. Le Bleuet is painted blue, while the Coquelicot is up under the eaves. Value-for-money evening meals could include local specialities such as *tourtes* (pies) or snails from a neighbouring farm. Walkers come in autumn, summer guests laze in deck-chairs in the large garden.

Directions 20 km SW of Sancerre. Take D 955. Turn left on D 44, go through Montigny to La Reculée. Signposted.

❖ La Reculée, 18250 Montigny **Tel** 48 69 59 18 **Rooms** 5
Prices FF **Evening meal** by request **Credit Cards** no
Children yes **Disabled** no **Pets** yes **Closed** never
Languages English **Proprietors** Jean-Louis and Elisabeth Gressin

Muides-sur-Loire, NE of Blois

Château de Colliers

Even though this is within easy reach of Chambord and other grand Loire Valley châteaux, it can be hard to drag yourself away from its own splendid views over the Loire. It can also be hard to drag yourself out of the particularly comfortable beds. The owner runs a mattress factory. In the dining-room, with its pretty grey wallpaper, the breakfast speciality is a warm *crêpe* with home-made jam. Riverside walks. Reserve well in advance.

Directions 20 km NE of Blois. Take D 951 along Loire. Signposted on left, before Muides.

❖ 41500 Muides-sur-Loire **Tel** 54 87 50 75 **Fax** 54 87 03 64 **Rooms** 5 **Prices** FFFF **Evening meal** by request **Credit Cards** no **Children** yes **Disabled** no **Pets** yes **Closed** never; telephone in winter **Languages** English, Spanish **Proprietors** M and Mme de Gelis

Nazelles-Négron, N of Amboise

La Huberdière

The former 17thC hunting lodge has quite a reputation but we were disappointed to find it looking down-at-heel. Although the bedrooms have private bathrooms, these are old-fashioned: some rather rustic, others large and traditional. Ernest Meissonnier, the bearded 19thC painter, was an ancestor. The hosts are friendly but the history, grounds, ornamental pond and home-cooking do not compensate for the lack of comfort and high prices.

Directions 1 km N of Amboise. Take D 31. Clearly marked north of the river.

❖37530 Nazelles-Négron **Tel** 47 57 39 32 **Fax** 47 23 15 79 **Rooms** 6 **Prices** FFF **Evening meal** by request **Credit Cards** no **Children** yes **Disabled** no **Pets** yes **Closed** never **Languages** English, Italian, Spanish **Proprietor** Béatrice Sandrier

Oizon, SE of Aubigny-sur-Nère

Château de la Verrerie

One of France's most famous châteaux is open for tours and, surprisingly, for bed-and-breakfast. There can be few more romantic spots: the mansion, reflected in the lake, was built 500 years ago by the Scottish Stuarts of Darnley. The antiques are museum-quality while the overall effect is as impressive as the prices. Is it worth the money? Decide for yourself. The Maison d'Hélène restaurant in the park is equally expensive.

Directions 15 km SE of Aubigny-sur-Nère. Take D 940; turn left on D 171, right at les Naudins, left on D 89 to château.

❖ Oizon, 18700 Aubigny-sur-Nère **Tel** 45 58 06 91
Fax 48 58 21 25 **Rooms** 12 **Prices** FFFF **Evening meal** no
Credit Cards MC V **Children** yes **Disabled** no **Pets** no
Closed never; telephone in winter **Languages** English, German
Proprietors Comte and Comtesse de Vogüé

Panzoult, E of Chinon

Domaine de Beauséjour

The Chinon wines produced by the Chauveau family have only been developed in the past 25 years, the guest rooms opened in 1991. Both businesses have considerable style. Two of the bedrooms, in a separate building next to the swimming-pool, have tiled floors, Persian rugs, antique furniture and firm mattresses on the beds. A suite is in the main house. All bathrooms are modern. Excellent base in Vienne valley.

Directions 12 km E of Chinon. Take D 21. Clearly signposted on left before Panzoult.

❖ 37220 Panzoult **Tel** 47 58 64 64 **Fax** 47 95 27 13 **Rooms** 3
Prices FFF **Evening meal** no **Credit Cards** no **Children** yes
Disabled no **Pets** yes **Closed** never **Languages** English; some
Italian, Spanish **Proprietors** Chauveau family

Paudy, SW of Vierzon

Château de Dangy

The Place family's handsome château has 18 rooms but only five are used for bed-and-breakfast. Romantic connections range from novelist George Sand to Grace Kelly, who both stayed here. There is even a distant link to the British royal family through Plantagenet ancestors. Lucie Place offers game from the Sologne (wild boar with cranberries) plus duck with olives from her native South. Reasonably priced bedrooms overlook parkland.

Directions 25 km SW of Vierzon. Take N 20. Turn left on D 16. In Paudy, follow signs for château, left on D 27.

❖ 36260 Paudy **Tel** 54 49 42 24 **Fax** 54 49 42 99 **Rooms** 5
Prices FFFF **Evening meal** by request **Credit Cards** no
Children yes **Disabled** no **Pets** no **Closed** never
Languages French only **Proprietors** M and Mme Place

La Possonnière, W of Angers

La Rousselière

Just above the Loire, this 16thC priory, rebuilt in the 19thC, has a colonial-looking veranda at the front of the house, overlooking a pretty garden. The comfortable bedrooms have names (Roses, Blue Dream): three have TV, minibar and their own telephones. The owner opened in 1992 and enjoys cooking with duck, Loire fish and fruit and vegetables from her large garden. There is also a full-sized billiard table plus an outdoor swimming-pool.

Directions 22 km W of Angers. N 23 to St-Georges-sur-Loire. Left on D 961, left on D 111. On left after 1.5 km. Signs.

❖ D 111, 49170 La Possonnière **Tel** 41 39 13 21 **Rooms** 4
Prices FF **Evening meal** by request **Credit Cards** no
Children yes **Disabled** no **Pets** yes **Closed** Nov **Languages** some
English **Proprietor** Jeanne Charpentier

Rigny-Ussé, E of Ussé

Le Pin

This L-shaped working farm belongs to the famous 'Sleeping Beauty' château of Ussé, 2 km away. The owners, who have lived here for 250 years, aim to keep families happy and busy, with a large swimming-pool, sauna, table tennis and billiards. The spacious, clean and comfortable bedrooms have straightforward decoration. A self-contained building has its own sitting-room, kitchenette and galleried bedroom upstairs, which makes it ideal for families. Restaurants nearby.

Directions 2 km E of Ussé. Signposted in village.

❖ 37420 Rigny-Ussé **Tel** 47 95 52 99 **Rooms** 4 **Prices** FF **Evening meal** by request in summer **Credit Cards** no **Children** yes **Disabled** no **Pets** yes **Closed** never **Languages** English **Proprietor** Jany Brousset

Roches-Prémarie, S of Poitiers

Château de Prémarie

With its fortified turrets and central courtyard, this is a real castle dating back to the 15thC. Today the spacious grounds include a tennis-court, swimming-pool and walled garden. Inside, rooms are predictably large but filled with old-fashioned rather than antique furniture. The wallpaper is rather dull; rugs lie on highly polished wood floors. The half-tiled bathrooms also have wood floors. The hosts are kind but the prices are somewhat expensive.

Directions 11 km S of Poitiers. Take D 741 towards Civray. Château is signposted on left at village.

❖ 86340 Roches-Prémarie **Tel** 49 42 50 01 **Rooms** 5 **Prices** FFF **Evening meal** no **Credit Cards** no **Children** yes **Disabled** no **Pets** no **Closed** Nov to Easter **Languages** English, German, Spanish **Proprietor** Jean-Pierre de Boysson

St-Denis-sur-Loire, E of Blois

La Closerie

On the outskirts of Blois, high above the Loire, this is a near-perfect bed-and-breakfast. The owner really enjoys having guests and her 17th and 18thC cottages are tastefully decorated. One faces a small swimming-pool. Breakfast is served here, outside in summer, inside when cool. Above, the spacious beamed bedroom has a modern bathroom. Cars are safe at night behind the entrance gate. Mme Herbinet is an expert on the area.

Directions 5 km E of Blois. N 152 for Orléans, then second right turning after St Denis. House is in hamlet of Les Mées.

❖ 3 rue de la Croix, Les Mées, 41000 St-Denis-sur-Loire
Tel 54 46 84 45 **Fax** 54 46 80 91 **Rooms** 3 **Prices** FFF
Evening meal no **Credit Cards** no **Children** yes **Disabled** no
Pets no **Closed** Dec to Feb **Languages** English, German
Proprietor Marie-Véronique Herbinet

St-Mathurin-sur-Loire, E of Angers

La Bouquetterie

Jolly window-boxes brighten the pale stone, handsome 19thC town house run by an enthusiastic couple with two young children. The brown-and-gold decoration is somewhat old-fashioned, but bedrooms are roomy with modern, well-fitted bathrooms. Guests may use a sitting-room which doubles as the dining-room where Claudine serves her reasonably priced meals using produce from their orchard and vegetable garden. Overlooks the Loire.

Directions 18 km E of Angers. Take D 952. At entry to village.

❖ 118 rue du Roi René, 49250 St-Mathurin-sur-Loire
Tel 41 57 02 00 **Rooms** 4 **Prices** FF **Evening meal** by request
Credit Cards V **Children** yes **Disabled** no **Pets** no **Closed** never
Languages English, some Italian **Proprietors** Claudine and
Christian Pinier

St-Michel-sur-Loire, W of Langeais

Château de Montbrun

One of the most expensive, and best, places in this guide. Michèle was a dancer, Ray a well-known singer; in 1992 they renovated the late 19thC château with its elegant garden. Old and new mix comfortably: black leather sofas by an old stone fireplace; a Persian rug on a black-and-white tiled floor; a modern painting above a carved sideboard. Bedrooms are feminine, with matching curtains and bedspreads. Dinners are an occasion.

Directions 4 km W of Langeais. Take N 152, D 125 through St-Michel-sur-Loire. Follow signs, beyond village.

❖ St-Michel-sur-Loire, 37130 Langeais **Tel and Fax** 47 96 57 13 **Rooms** 5 **Prices** FFFF **Evening meal** by request **Credit Cards** no **Children** no **Disabled** no **Pets** no **Closed** late Feb to mid-March **Languages** English, Italian **Proprietors** Michèle and Ray Gentès

St-Nicolas-de-Bourgueil, NE of Saumur

Domaine du Fondis

The elegant limestone town house with its small courtyard is well-maintained but seems to lack warmth. The bedrooms are named after grape varieties: Groslot, Chenin, Sauvignon and Cabernet but have a bland, hotel-like quality with few personal touches, though there are some antiques. Bathrooms are modern and clean. Views are over the owner's own vineyards. Verdict: a clean, well-priced, convenient overnight stop in a popular region.

Directions 22 km NE of Saumur. Take N 147 N, then D 10 E. House is signposted on edge of village.

❖ Le Fondis, 37140 St-Nicolas-de-Bourgueil **Tel** 47 97 78 58 **Fax** 47 97 43 59 **Rooms** 4 **Prices** FF **Evening meal** no **Credit Cards** no **Children** yes **Disabled** no **Pets** no **Closed** never; telephone in winter **Languages** some English **Proprietor** Martine Jamet

Savonnières, W of Tours

10 rue Chaude

Step through the gate into the courtyard of this creeper-clad 15thC cottage and 'you are in another world'. The owner first welcomed guests in 1988. Rooms are atmospheric and unspoiled, except the bathrooms, of course. A loom stands in the corner of one of the two bedrooms, linked by a common bathroom. Lucette Care never lets both bedrooms, except to friends or a family. A special experience, near Villandry.

Directions 13 km W of Tours. Take D 7 to village. Rue Chaude is lane on left.

❖ 10 rue Chaude, 37510 Savonnières **Tel** 47 50 03 26 **Rooms** 2 **Prices** FF **Evening meal** no **Credit Cards** no **Children** yes **Disabled** no **Pets** no **Closed** Nov to mid-Feb **Languages** French only **Proprietor** Lucette Care

Selles-sur-Cher, S of Blois

Maison de la Rive Gauche

The scene looks French: behind the tall iron railings, a cat sleeps in a tiny garden on a narrow side street. But the lady watering the flowers is English as is the informality of the three-storey 16thC house in the old part of Selles. Of the six bedrooms, one is a single, another sleeps four. Guests may relax in the sitting-room or in the rear courtyard where a small cottage is rented for self-catering holidays. Excellent touring base for Loire châteaux.

Directions 41 km S of Blois. Take D 956 to Selles-sur-Cher; on south bank near château.

❖ 15 rue du Four, 41130 Selles-sur-Cher **Tel** 54 97 63 85 **Rooms** 6 **Prices** FF **Evening meal** by request **Credit Cards** no **Children** yes **Disabled** no **Pets** no **Closed** never **Languages** English, German **Proprietor** Mrs I Bacon

Château de Ternay

For those seeking a real château experience: parts date from the 12thC and there is even a Gothic chapel. The de Ternays played a role in both French and American naval history but today's descendants are a relaxed couple who make goats' cheeses on the estate. The rooms are crammed with antiques, the walls covered in old oil paintings. Nowadays, the owners' grown-up children host the evening meals.
Directions 12 km W of Loudun. Take D 14. Château on right before village.

❖ 86120 Ternay **Tel** 49 22 92 82 **Rooms** 3 **Prices** FFFF
Evening meal by request **Credit Cards** no **Children** yes
Disabled no **Pets** no **Closed** mid-Nov to Easter
Languages English **Proprietors** Marquis and Marquise de Ternay

Vernou-sur-Brenne, E of Tours

Château de Jallanges

Here you can actually stay in a Loire Valley château – a Renaissance gem with a vast courtyard and endless grounds. The bedrooms have recently been tastefully refurbished by the owner; while they retain many original features and antique furniture, beds are modern and firm. Bathrooms are also modern, spacious and bright. Weddings, conferences and art exhibitions are held in the impressive salons. The son is a chef. An expensive experience.
Directions 15 km E of Tours. Take N 152 to Vouvray, then D 46 to Vernou-sur-Brenne. Signposted.

❖ Vallée de Vaugondy, 37210 Vernou-sur-Brenne
Tel 47 52 01 71 **Fax** 47 52 11 18 **Rooms** 5 **Prices** FFFF
Evening meal by request **Credit Cards** no **Children** yes
Disabled no **Pets** yes **Closed** never **Languages** English, German
Proprietors Ferry-Balin family

➡ *More on page 172*

Les Abrets, W of Chambéry

La Bruyère

This looks like a traditional farmhouse but the interior is strictly contemporary: black directors' chairs in the dining-room, a low Japanese table in the sitting-room. Evening meals are special. Claude Chavalle, from the Côte d'Azur, prepares *bouillabaisse* and *choucroûte de poisson*. One bedroom is black-and-white with grey carpet and black bedside lights; all are light, with king-sized beds and named after the fabrics on the walls.

Directions 35 km W of Chambéry. Take A 43 to Chimilin-Les Abrets exit; D 592 to Les Abrets; after La Libarde, follow signs.

❖ La Bruyère, 38490 Les Abrets **Tel** 76 32 01 66 **Fax** 76 32 06 66
Rooms 7 **Prices** FFF **Evening meal** by request
Credit Cards MC V **Children** yes **Disabled** no **Pets** yes
Closed never **Languages** English **Proprietors** Claude and
Christian Chavalle

Andelot, N of Bourg-en-Bresse

Château d'Andelot

American money transformed this 12thC castle into a de luxe version of a medieval hideaway. Vast bedrooms have canopy beds with luxury mattresses; tiled bathrooms have Italian towels. Chandeliers rival Murano glass wall lights in the dining-room where gourmet meals are served by candlelight. The billiard-room at the top also sports pinball machines. Manageress Nathalie Roz offers to prepare picnics and there is a tennis-court.

Directions 36 km N of Bourg-en-Bresse. Take N 83 towards Lons-le-Saunier. Turn right at St-Amour on D 3 for Andelot.

❖ 39320 Andelot **Tel** 84 85 41 49 **Rooms** 6 **Prices** FFFF
Evening meal by request **Credit Cards** MC V **Children** yes
Disabled no **Pets** no **Closed** Dec to April
Languages English **Proprietor** Harry Bellin

Bligny-sur-Ouche, W of Beaune

Château d'Ecutigny

Dating from the 12th-17thC, this is an impressive building with a steep red-tiled roof. Bedrooms are grand: the honeymoon suite has a four-poster bed with gold bedspread and a circular sitting-room in the tower with a sofa, a stereo and a fireplace. Imaginative breakfasts could include *fromage frais* with a raspberry *coulis* and fruit salad. Dinner is very expensive: local favourites such as *coq au vin* or *poulet à la crème*.

Directions 28 km W of Beaune. Take D 970 to Bligny, then D 33 to Ecutigny. Château is on right, past church.

❖ Ecutigny, 21360 Bligny-sur-Ouche **Tel** 80 20 19 14
Fax 80 20 19 15 **Rooms** 6 **Prices** FFFF **Evening meal** by request
Credit Cards MC V **Children** yes **Disabled** no **Pets** yes
Closed never **Languages** English, Spanish
Proprietors Françoise and Patrick Rochet

Bourg d'Oisans, SE of Grenoble

Les Petites Sources

Eric Durdan, a qualified mountain guide, leads climbing, off-piste skiing and snowshoe expeditions in the Ecrins Range. His converted barn is like a comfortable ski chalet (though Alpe d'Huez is 15 km away). Furniture is mainly modern and wooden, though dried flowers decorate an old sideboard. Bedrooms have pine panels and doors, bathrooms are small. Three kinds of bread at breakfast and *gratin dauphinois* at supper: this is the simple life.

Directions 50 km SE of Grenoble via N 85, N 91. Le Vert is 1.8 km S of middle of town along Chemin du Paradis.

❖ Le Vert, 38520 Bourg d'Oisans **Tel** 76 80 13 92 **Rooms** 6
Prices FF **Evening meal** by request **Credit Cards** V **Children** yes
Disabled yes **Pets** yes **Closed** never **Languages** English
Proprietors Pauline and Eric Durdan

Buxy, SW of Chalon-sur-Saône

Château de Sassangy

Our inspector was impressed by this carefully restored 18thC château with vineyards, chestnut trees and coloured, glazed roof tiles. Inside, Chinese vases flank marble fire-places; the owner upholsters much of the silk-covered furniture herself. The dining-room has a vaulted ceiling; the dark wood library is more grand than comfortable. The bedrooms are furnished with quality fabrics and antiques.

Directions SW of Chalon-sur-Saône. N 80, D 981 to Buxy. D 977 to Sassangy. Signposted in village.

❖ 71390 Buxy **Tel** 85 96 12 40 **Fax** 85 96 11 44 **Rooms** 6 **Prices** FFFF **Evening meal** by request **Credit Cards** MC V **Children** no **Disabled** no **Pets** no **Closed** mid-Nov to mid-March **Languages** English **Proprietors** M and Mme Marceau

Chamboeuf, SW of Dijon

Le Relais de Chasse

'You think you're driving up to a farm, but the main building is a former hunting lodge with a steep, grey-tiled roof.' Two huge cedars and a yew stand guard. The best bedroom overlooks the garden: black floral curtains match armchairs, the bathroom is small but pretty. Families use two vast, connecting bedrooms that share a bathroom: the parent's room boasts a piano. 'Comfortable but not too posh', it is somewhat expensive.

Directions 17 km SW of Dijon. Take N 74 to Gevrey-Chambertin. Turn right on D 31 to village. Follow signs.

❖ 21220 Chamboeuf **Tel** 80 51 81 60 **Fax** 80 34 15 96 **Rooms** 4 **Prices** FFF **Evening meal** no **Credit Cards** no **Children** yes **Disabled** no **Pets** no **Closed** never **Languages** English **Proprietor** Michelle Girard

Chasse-sur-Rhône, NW of Vienne

Domaine de Gorneton

Set round a leafy courtyard, this 17thC mansion has been a family home for 30 years. Antiques add to the ambience of the heavily beamed dining-room and sitting-room. A favourite bedroom is Les Lions which is on two levels joined by a spiral staircase. Dinner is an event, with regional classics and is worth the money. Swimming-pool, tennis-court and, most of all, the Fleitous' hospitality make this special.

Directions 10 km NW of Vienne. Exit A 7 at Chasse-sur-Rhône; pass stadium, cross railway lines, head for Trembas. House on right.

❖ Hameau de Trembas, 38670 Chasse-sur-Rhône
Tel and Fax 72 24 19 15 **Rooms** 3 **Prices** FFFF **Evening meal** by request **Credit Cards** no **Children** yes **Disabled** no **Pets** no **Closed** never **Languages** English, Spanish, some German **Proprietors** Jean and Jacqueline Fleitou

Châtenay, S of Charolles

Lavaux

Ducks and cows made way for a *ferme-auberge* and bedrooms when two sides of a traditional farm courtyard were converted. The busy owners live in between. The latest and largest bedroom is in a tower with rural antique furniture to complement the beams. Evening meals are above average: *poulet à la crème* and *gâteau de foie de volaille*, a hot chicken liver mousse. Children can pet the animals, bike and fish in the pond.

Directions 27 km S of Charolles. Take D 985; left at la Clayette on D 987; left on D 300 to Châtenay. House beyond village.

❖ 71800 Châtenay **Tel** 85 28 08 48 **Rooms** 5 **Prices** FF **Evening meal** yes; closed Tues **Credit Cards** no **Children** yes **Disabled** no **Pets** no **Closed** mid-Nov to Easter **Languages** English **Proprietor** Paulette Gelin

Château de Chorey-lès-Beaune

'Beautiful but not too awe-inspiring', this moated château is famous for its Premier Cru wines. The rooms are enormous: the dining-room has space to spare even with two large tables. The bedrooms, with high, beamed ceilings, are comfortable, not too posh. One has a yellow colour scheme: floor-to-ceiling curtains, chair and patchwork quilt. Beds have massive wooden head and footboards. Bathrooms are bright and modern. Expensive.
Directions 3 km NE of Beaune. Take N 74 towards Dijon. Chorey is 1 km off N 74, on right.

❖ Chorey-lès-Beaune, 21200 Beaune **Tel** 80 22 06 05
Fax 80 24 03 93 **Rooms** 6 **Prices** FFFF **Evening meal** no
Credit Cards MC V **Children** yes **Disabled** no **Pets** yes
Closed Dec to March **Languages** English, German
Proprietors M and Mme François Germain

La Vieille Auberge

Only 6 km from the most famous wine road in the world, this modest village stands among fields. In 1990, the Plimmers, a young English couple, converted the old village inn into a plain, practical, informal but comfortable halt. The 'hangar-like' dining-room, decorated with wine maps, has a billiard table up a few steps. Jane prepares French dishes: pork with Dijon mustard, *crème brûlée* with raspberries from her garden. Bedrooms somewhat bare.
Directions 22 km S of Dijon. Take D 996; bear right on D 109 after Saulon-la-Rue. House is on village green.

❖ Epernay-sous-Gevrey, 21220 Gevrey-Chambertin
Tel 80 36 61 76 **Fax** 80 36 64 68 **Rooms** 5 **Prices** FF
Evening meal by request **Credit Cards** no **Children** yes
Disabled no **Pets** no **Closed** Christmas **Languages** English
Proprietors Jules and Jane Plimmer

Les Buissonnets

'A useful base for wine-lovers' since Rully, Mercurey and Givry are just minutes from this elegant, low house. 'American-style' decorations include tartan ribbons on the banisters. Bedrooms are comfortable with walk-in wardrobes. Some have dressing tables; the best look over the walled garden. Bathrooms are small but have fluffy towels. The highlight is Madame's Burgundian cooking: *poulet à la crème, boeuf bourguignonne.*

Directions 13 km NW of Chalon-sur-Saône. Take D 978 W; D 981 towards Chagny. Fontaines is off to right. House in middle.

❖ 102 Grande Rue, 71150 Fontaines **Tel** 85 91 48 49 **Rooms** 5
Prices FFF **Evening meal** by request **Credit Cards** MC V
Children yes **Disabled** no **Pets** yes **Closed** never
Languages English **Proprietors** Jacotte and Michel Chignac

la Guiche, S of Montceau-les-Mines

La Roseraie

No prizes for guessing the host's nationality: a neat lawn with flowers planted in a wheelbarrow; English furniture inside; even the name, La Roseraie, is 'English humour', a play on the name of owner Ros Binns. Once past the impressive gateway to this pretty country house, informality reigns: guests often wander into the kitchen, though after three years, Ros stopped offering dinner since "there are so many good, small restaurants nearby".

Directions 25 km S of Montceau-les-Mines. Take D 980; turn right on D 33; D 27 to middle of quiet village.

❖ 71220 la Guiche **Tel** 85 24 67 82 **Fax** 85 24 61 03 **Rooms** 4
Prices FFF **Evening meal** no **Credit Cards** no **Children** yes
Disabled no **Pets** yes **Closed** never **Languages** English, Spanish
Proprietors Ros and John Binns

Château de Bois-Franc

On a hill in the Beaujolais vineyards, this Napoleon III château has sumptuous reception rooms used for conferences, so the ambience is business-like rather than warm and friendly. We can only recommend the more expensive, two-bedroom suite with a high ceiling, curtains tied with gold tassels plus a modern bathroom in grey and white. The other suite smells musty and has an antiquated WC and shower. An expensive experience.

Directions 9 km W of Villefranche-sur-Saône. Take D 38, turn right on D 31 via Chervinges. Jarnioux is on left, château signposted.

❖ 69640 Jarnioux **Tel** 74 68 20 91 **Fax** 74 65 10 03 **Rooms** 2 **Prices** FFFF **Evening meal** no **Credit Cards** no **Children** yes **Disabled** no **Pets** yes **Closed** never **Languages** English, German **Proprietors** M and Mme Doat

Longecourt-en-Plaine, SE of Dijon

Château de Longecourt

The enthusiasm and welcome of this hostess is a model for other château owners. Her moated and turreted mansion, redesigned by Lenoir in 1760, is grand but not overpowering. The echoing dining-room has pillars, stencilled walls and a circular table. Bedrooms in the tower are vast: one has a piano. 'Venise' has stencils of cats and Venice. Bathrooms are small but modern. Evening meals are delicious but expensive.

Directions 17 km SE of Dijon. Take D 968 along Burgundy Canal. Château signposted in village on left.

❖ Longecourt-en-Plaine, 21110 Genlis **Tel** 80 39 88 76 **Rooms** 4 **Prices** FFFF **Evening meal** by request **Credit Cards** AE **Children** yes **Disabled** yes **Pets** yes **Closed** never **Languages** English, German, Italian, Spanish **Proprietors** Comte and Comtesse de St-Seine

Chez Dumay

The owners' home is a former wine grower's house; in a separate building an outside staircase leads to bedrooms with floral wallpaper and net curtains. These are comfortable enough but the bathrooms need of a facelift. Breakfast is in the rather sombre dining-room with French windows opening on to the garden. In the hall are tourist pamphlets plus local honey, soap, sweets and mustard for sale. The hosts are 'a sweet, middle-aged couple'.

Directions 11 km N of Beaune. Take N 74; left on D 115 to Magny. At end of lane behind the church.

❖ 21700 Magny-lès-Villers **Tel** 80 62 91 16 **Rooms** 3 **Prices** FF **Evening meal** no **Credit Cards** no **Children** yes **Disabled** no **Pets** no **Closed** never **Languages** English, German **Proprietors** Robert and Micheline Dumay

---

Mens, S of Grenoble

rue du Bourg

'Somebody I'd go back to visit,' says our inspector who felt at home in this remote mountain village thanks to Mme Fribourg's welcome. The house is 17th-19thC with low ceilings, beams and a curving staircase. The bedroom at the top, with triangular windows and a hanging basket of petunias, looks over the old tiled roofs of the village. Dinner using local produce is excellent value, including aperitif, wine and coffee. Breakfasts, too, are hearty.

Directions 58 km S of Grenoble. Take N 85 to la Mure. Turn right on D 526, twisting road to Mens.

❖ rue du Bourg, 38710 Mens **Tel** 76 34 60 14 **Rooms** 6 **Prices** FF **Evening meal** by request **Credit Cards** no **Children** yes **Disabled** no **Pets** yes **Closed** never **Languages** English, Italian **Proprietor** Pierrette Fribourg

Montcet, W of Bourg-en-Bresse

Les Vignes

These hosts are unusual: psychoanalyst Jean-Louis Gayet holds meditation sessions; he also builds microlights. Eliane specialises in vegetarian dishes using organic produce; 'the seaweed flan with raspberry *coulis* is delicious'. Rooms have hypo-allergenic beds with special mattresses. In a tranquil setting, this restored farmhouse has a pond, large garden and no neighbours. Rooms are sparsely furnished; there is a 'kid's room' for rainy days.

Directions 12 km W of Bourg-en-Bresse. Take D 936; turn right on D 45 through Montcet towards Vendeins. House on right.

❖ 01310 Montcet **Tel** 74 24 23 13 **Rooms** 4 **Prices** FF **Evening meal** by request **Credit Cards** no **Children** yes **Disabled** no **Pets** no **Closed** never **Languages** English, Spanish, Esperanto **Proprietors** Jean-Louis and Eliane Gayet

Montmaur, W of Gap

Château de Montmaur

For 20 years, the preservation of this ancient château has been a labour of love for the owners and their seven daughters, financed by guided tours and wedding receptions. One Renaissance room has massive beams, murals and an imposing fireplace. Bedrooms, all suites, are in the 12thC wing: cool in summer, with a minimum of decoration, some have co-ordinated paisley wallpaper and bedspreads, velvet-covered chairs. Bathrooms are immaculate.

Directions 22 km W of Gap. Take D 994. Montmaur is on right. Château stands out.

❖ Montmaur, 05400 Veynes **Tel** 92 58 11 42 **Rooms** 5 **Prices** FFF **Evening meal** no **Credit Cards** no **Children** yes **Disabled** no **Pets** yes **Closed** never **Languages** English **Proprietors** Raymond and Elise Laurens

Montvalezan, E of Bourg-St-Maurice

Chalet Rosière

What looks like a classic mountain-side Savoie chalet outside has been 'reversed' inside by the British owners, who converted the hay loft into a huge room. Picture windows open on to the wooden balcony with panoramic views. There is a library, sitting-room, dining-room and kitchen on the top floor. The hosts advise where the best snow is and have an excellent local guide. Just below small ski resort of La Rosière La Thiule.

Directions 10 km E of Bourg-St-Maurice. D 902; left to La Rosière; through Montvalezan to Les Laix 1440. Last house on left.

❖ Les Laix, 73700 Montvalezan **Tel** 79 06 81 99; London (0171) 584 7435 **Rooms** 2 **Prices** FF **Evening meal** yes **Credit Cards** no **Children** yes **Disabled** no **Pets** yes **Closed** Easter to Nov **Languages** English **Proprietors** Charles and Ardie Volkers

Morancé, NW of Lyon

Domaine des Tessonnières

Just above the village, this friendly couple are *viticulteurs-récoltants*, growing and making their own *appellation contrôlée* Beaujolais. Guests can taste and buy in their *cave* (cellar) with its ancient winepress. The attractive stone house has a terrace at the front used for breakfast in summer. The sole bedroom has twin beds, a beamed ceiling, a terracotta floor, small balcony and modern, bright bathroom. The evening meal is well-priced.

Directions 20 km NW of Lyon. Take N 6, then D 485 to Civrieux. Turn on to D 30; left into Morancé. House on left past cemetery.

❖ 69480 Morancé **Tel** 74 67 02 70 **Rooms** 1 **Prices** FF **Evening meal** by request **Credit Cards** no **Children** yes **Disabled** no **Pets** yes **Closed** grape harvest Sept, Oct **Languages** French only **Proprietors** Annick and Michel Ravet

la Motte Ternant, NE of Saulieu

Le Presbytère

A French architect renovated the 15thC presbytery by the 11thC church; a French interior designer put up the curtains; evening meals feature grilled goats' cheese, *boeuf bourguignonne, coq au vin* and, because the owners are British, blackberry and apple crumble. They are happy to suggest Côte d'Or wine producers for guests who enjoy tasting. The garden is large enough to find a private secluded spot. Marjorie even serves a light lunch.
Directions 10 km NE of Saulieu. Take D 26 to village. Next to church.

❖ la Motte Ternant, 21210 Saulieu **Tel** 80 84 34 85
Fax 80 84 35 32 **Rooms** 3 **Prices** FF **Evening meal** by request
Credit Cards no **Children** not small ones **Disabled** no **Pets** no
Closed never **Languages** English **Proprietors** Marjorie and
Brian Aylett

Queige, N of Albertville

Le Villaret

Hay is cut by hand and chickens roam freely at this organic mountain farm. Bread, cheese and eggs feature at meals. The airy dining-room has wooden skis and Winter Olympic mascots on the walls. Mt Blanc is framed in the glass doorway leading to the balcony. Cosy bedrooms have sloping pine ceilings, wicker furniture, simple decorations and clean, tidy bathrooms. Mme Poire enjoys telling guests about undiscovered places. All very healthy.
Directions 6 km N of Albertville. Take the twisting D 925. Queige is on left. Follow signs to Les Côtes.

❖ Les Côtes, 73720 Queige **Tel** 79 38 02 69 **Rooms** 5
Prices FFF **Evening meal** by request **Credit Cards** no
Children yes **Disabled** yes **Pets** yes **Closed** never
Languages English, German, Italian **Proprietor** Marcel Poire

Quincié-en-Beaujolais, W of Belleville

Domaine de Romarand

Winemakers Jean and Annie Berthelot redecorated three bedrooms for guests in 1992. Flowery bedspreads match curtains;
water-colours hang on pink or blue walls; bathrooms are small and
bright. The rustic dining-room has beams, stone walls, and a large
table for traditional meals featuring *boeuf bourguignonne, salade lyon-
naise*. The swimming-pool is a bonus; the dogs and free-range
chickens make it very 'farmy'.

Directions 12 km W of Belleville. Take D 37; turn left on D 9. Go
through Quincié and look for signs.

❖ 69430 Quincié-en-Beaujolais **Tel** 74 04 34 49 **Rooms** 3
Prices FF **Evening meal** by request **Credit Cards** no
Children yes **Disabled** no **Pets** yes **Closed** never
Languages English **Proprietors** Jean and Annie Berthelot

Rotalier, S of Lons-le-Saunier

Château Gréa

Ancient floorboards squeak in the hall of this 250-year-old country
mansion dominated by huge cedars. Breakfast, served in the dining-room, can include cheese or bacon and eggs. A glass-fronted
cabinet displays old English china. One bedroom has thick white
curtains and a huge private bathroom with a high-sided bath. A
corridor and bathroom link the other two bedrooms, one with
bunk beds. The family here are a delight.

Directions 10 km S of Lons-le-Saunier. Take N 83 towards Bourg-
en-Bresse. Turn left for Rotalier. Follow signs.

❖ 39190 Rotalier **Tel** 84 25 05 07 **Rooms** 3 **Prices** FFF
Evening meal no **Credit Cards** no **Children** yes **Disabled** no
Pets yes **Closed** never **Languages** English, Spanish
Proprietors Pierre and Bénédicte de Boissieu

La Combe Fleurie

Scotsman Donald Clark, who runs the lifts at a nearby ski resort, married local girl Agnès and built their home in 1993. Light and airy, with a mixture of rustic and modern furniture, the house is 'informal, like a ski chalet'. Bedrooms have beige floor tiles, pine beds and modern lights. One, in the roof, has five singles and a double. The well-priced dinner features hearty local dishes such as *tourton* (potato pie). Not for those seeking old-world charm.

Directions 14 km N of Gap. Take N 85. St-Bonnet is on D 43, off on right. House is through village on left, signposted.

❖ route de Chaillol, 05500 St-Bonnet **Tel** 92 50 53 97 **Fax** 92 50 18 28 **Rooms** 6 **Prices** FF **Evening meal** by request **Credit Cards** V **Children** yes **Disabled** no **Pets** yes **Closed** never **Languages** English, Spanish **Proprietors** Donald and Agnès Clark

Sennecy-le-Grand, N of Tournus

Le Clos des Tourelles

The owner is a talented cook and dinner is served in what was once a medieval armoury. Stone paving, heavy beams and a monumental fireplace make a dramatic setting for fish stew or *gâteau de saumon fumé*. Above-average food at above-average prices. In a separate Mâcon-style building with a long wooden balcony are the bedrooms. Elegant and uncluttered, they have evocative names such as Mata Hari, and late-19thC furniture.

Directions 10 km N of Tournus. Take N 6. The château is signposted in town.

❖ Château de la Tour, 71240 Sennecy-le-Grand **Tel** 85 44 83 95 **Fax** 85 44 90 18 **Rooms** 6 **Prices** FFF **Evening meal** by request **Credit Cards** V **Children** yes **Disabled** no **Pets** no **Closed** Dec, Jan **Languages** English **Proprietor** Laurence Derruder

L'Alpillonne

Full marks for being different. Every corner of this 200-year-old house has reminders of the good old days. Above the beds in the rather frilly Hirondelles bedroom hang a his-and-hers top hat and bonnet; the Fenière has more straw hats and a small, barred window. We prefer the Pigeonniers with its fun bathroom and broad balcony. Well-priced meals are in the Bergerie, an old sheep-shed. Swimming-pool. Some traffic noise in garden, but most guests are happy to put up with this.

Directions 3 km N of Serres on right side of N 75.

❖ La Plaine de Sigottier, 05700 Serres **Tel** 92 67 08 98 **Rooms** 5
Prices FF **Evening meal** by request **Credit Cards** no
Children yes **Disabled** no **Pets** yes **Closed** Oct to mid-June
Languages English **Proprietors** Gilberte and Emile Moynier

Torchefelon, W of Chambéry

Le Colombier

Food is the attraction in this peach and pastel green house. Nicole Pignoly's meals could include chicken with crayfish, pigeon with *foie gras* or sweetbreads with mushrooms. She also packs elaborate picnics for guests who drive about the countryside in the pony and trap. The bedrooms are plain and old-fashioned but the sunny terrace has a pergola and geraniums. Children like the plethora of dogs, cats, doves and horses.

Directions 50 km W of Chambéry. Exit A 43 at la Tour-du-Pin; take D 51; just before Doissin take right to Torchefelon; follow signs.

❖ La Taillat 38690 Torchefelon **Tel** 74 92 29 28 **Fax** 74 92 27 33
Rooms 3 **Prices** FF **Evening meal** by request **Credit Cards** no
Children yes **Disabled** no **Pets** yes **Closed** never
Languages French only **Proprietors** Nicole and Jean-Pierre Pignoly

Tournus

33 quai du Midi

Overlooking the Saône River, this 200-year-old town house is attractive with cream shutters, pink walls, and flowerbeds. The bedrooms are particularly well-furnished. One has a four-poster bed curtained in primrose yellow with a burgundy and gold frieze and two armchairs. Bathrooms are small, clean and practical. There is a billiard-room and a boat for hire. The owner, who moved here in 1990, could be a little more cordial. On the other hand, good in-town *chambres d'hôtes* are to be encouraged.
Directions down by the Saône River in Tournus.

❖ 33 quai du Midi, 71700 Tournus **Tel** 85 51 78 65
Fax 85 40 02 67 **Rooms** 4 **Prices** FF **Evening meal** no
Credit Cards no **Children** yes **Disabled** no **Pets** yes **Closed** never
Languages English, German, Italian **Proprietor** Solange Bouret

Villard-de-Lans, SW of Grenoble

La Croix du Liorin

Guy Bertrand is an architect; his circular house is 'in the middle of nowhere', 1250 m above sea level. Outdoor folk return year after year, to cross-country ski, mountain bike and hike the trails in the nearby forest. The dining/sitting/kitchen area is open-plan with a central wood-burning stove. Both bedrooms are on the ground floor; one has a loft with a ladder for children to reach their beds. Bathrooms are simple, food is regional.
Directions 35 km SW of Grenoble. Take N 532, D 531 to Villard-de-Lans. Follow D 215 to Bois Barbu and look for signs.

❖ Bois Barbu, 38250 Villard-de-Lans **Tel** 76 95 82 67
Fax 76 95 85 75 **Rooms** 2 **Prices** FF **Evening meal** by request
Credit Cards no **Children** yes **Disabled** yes **Pets** no
Closed never **Languages** French only **Proprietors** Nicole and Guy Bertrand

Villard-de-Lans, SW of Grenoble

La Ferme les Quatre Vents

For holidaymakers looking for a Heidi-like experience in an old alpine farmhouse (altitude 1120 m). Water runs through a stone trough; cows are a part of everyday life. Set away from the village, with lawn, orchards and meadows. Open according to seasonal demand: winter brings skiers who use the nearby resort; spring attracts hikers; families come in summer holidays. The low prices of rooms and food are a genuine attraction.

Directions 34 km SW of Genoble. N 532, D 531 to Villard; D 215 to Bois Barbu. Right at church; signposted on right.

❖ Bois Barbu, 38250 Villard-de-Lans **Tel** 76 95 10 68 **Rooms** 5 **Prices** FF **Evening meal** by request **Credit Cards** no **Children** yes **Disabled** no **Pets** no **Closed** Oct, Nov; April: must telephone **Languages** English **Proprietor** Reine Uzel

Villard-de-Lans, SW of Grenoble

Le Val Ste-Marie

A traditional bed-and-breakfast where the Bon family offers guests the simple things in life. Hike or cross-country ski from the door of their secluded mountain farmhouse. Logs are stacked by the door of this wood-and-stone restoration which has plenty of flowery fabrics to brighten the interior. Mme Bon makes all her own soups, *pâtisserie* and uses local *charcuterie*. Pine abounds in the bedrooms which are unpretentiously rustic.

Directions 35 km SW of Grenoble. Take N 532, D 53 to Villard-de-Lans. Follow D 215 to Bois Barbu and look for signs.

❖ Bois Barbu, 38250 Villard-de-Lans **Tel** 76 95 92 80 **Fax** 76 95 56 79 **Rooms** 3 **Prices** FF **Evening meal** by request **Credit Cards** no **Children** yes **Disabled** no **Pets** no **Closed** never **Languages** English **Proprietors** Agnès and Dominique Bon

Villers-Robert, S of Dole

Le Moulin

This 200-year-old brick mill by a stream is surrounded by trees and fields. One comfortable, ground-floor bedroom has television, sofas in front of the fireplace and its own door to the terrace and garden. Guests sit at one table in the beamed dining-room with its purple wall-hangings. Choose the cheaper, lighter menu or a well-priced meal of home-made terrine, roast duck, salad and dessert. Open since 1993, the owner is still cool with guests.

Directions 17 km S of Dole. Take D 475. Turn left in le Deschaux on D 469. Mill is on stream before Villers-Robert.

❖ 39120 Villers-Robert **Tel** 84 71 52 39 **Rooms** 3 **Prices** FF **Evening meal** by request **Credit Cards** no **Children** yes **Disabled** yes **Pets** no **Closed** never **Languages** English **Proprietor** Jacqueline Monamy

Vosne-Romanée, S of Dijon

La Closerie des Ormes

Surrounded by high walls and tall trees, the ivy-covered house feels totally private. The owners, who opened up in 1993, have a love affair with Laura Ashley fabrics which appear in every room. Bedrooms have themes and names: Les Chats has cats painted on the white wall; La Bécassine features puppets, like a child's room; Chapeau has hats everywhere and a bath **in** the bedroom. Breakfast is taken seriously: white linen, eggs, cheese, *pain d'épice.*

Directions 22 km S of Dijon. Take N 74. House is at the north end of the village. Signposted.

❖ 21 rue de la Grand-Velle, 21700 Vosne-Romanée **Tel** 80 61 20 24 **Fax** 80 61 19 63 **Rooms** 3 **Prices** FFF **Evening meal** no **Credit Cards** no **Children** yes **Disabled** yes **Pets** no **Closed** Dec to March **Languages** English **Proprietors** Claude and Jean-Paul Grimm

 ➥ *More on page 178*

Artigueloutan, E of Pau

Château St-Jean

An iron gate leads to a tidy garden with hydrangeas, a magnolia tree and the creeper-clad building with mock fortifications. Up a flight of stairs, the sky-blue breakfast room has individual tables. There are shiny wooden floors throughout. The stylish bedrooms have plain walls with matching floral curtains and bedspreads; bathrooms are small, but modern. The owners run the restaurant nearby but the swimming-pool is for guests only. Comfortable.
Directions 8 km E of Pau. Take N 117, right on D 215. House is through village, past stadium, on left.

1 rue de l'Eglise, 64420 Artigueloutan **Tel** 59 81 84 30 **Rooms** 3
Prices FFF **Evening meal** no **Credit Cards** AE V **Children** yes
Disabled no **Pets** no **Closed** 2 weeks Feb **Languages** English
Proprietors Christiane and Patrice Nicaise

Baleyssagues, NW of Duras

Savary

A terrace with yellow and white awning overlooks the swimming-pool. The house itself has original stone floors and partly dates from the 12thC. The rustic look prevails: plain walls, solid new pine beds and firm mattresses. A medieval inglenook fireplace dominates the dining-room with its beams and long, communal table. The offer of a 'Dutch' breakfast of cheese and sausage reflects the origins of Hanneke and Chris.
Directions below Duras château, take turning for Bordepaille, D 134. After 2 km, turn right for Savary. House is second on right.

❖ Baleyssagues, 47120 Duras **Tel** 53 83 77 82 **Rooms** 5
Prices FF **Evening meal** by request **Credit Cards** no
Children yes **Disabled** no **Pets** no **Closed** Oct to mid-April
Languages English, German, Dutch **Proprietors** Chris and
Hanneke Schaepman

Bazas

Château d'Arbieu

Surrounded by meadows, this has been the family home for 300 years but the welcome and comfort are contemporary. 'The whole house is clean, highly polished and elegant; the gardens are well-kept'. Large bedrooms have firm beds and rugs on wood floors. Guests share the owners' sitting-room with its antiques and family portraits; Mme uses produce from their farm for dinner, served at the long table. An agreeable taste of 'château life'.

Directions 1 km SE of Bazas. Leave on D 655 and look for signs on right to Arbieu.

❖ 33430 Bazas **Tel** 56 25 11 18 **Fax** 56 25 90 52 **Rooms** 5 **Prices** FFF **Evening meal** by request **Credit Cards** AE MC V **Children** yes **Disabled** no **Pets** no **Closed** mid-Dec to mid-Jan **Languages** English **Proprietors** M and Mme Philippe de Chenerilles

Bosdarros, S of Pau

Maison Trille

The owner remodelled a 300-year-old house, installed electric heating, fine furniture and now has a handsome, tasteful home. The sitting-room has a card table, comfortable chairs and, off to one side, a twin-bedded room suitable for disabled access. Breakfast and dinner are served at individual tables. A courtyard behind has a barbecue and table tennis. Guests have use of a washing-machine. Not suitable for children. Highly recommended.

Directions 10 km S of Pau. Take N 134, then D 934 at Gan. House is 3.5 km on left behind Le Tucq restaurant.

❖ chemin de Labau, route de Rébénacq, 64290 Bosdarros **Tel** 59 21 79 51 **Fax** 59 21 66 98 **Rooms** 5 **Prices** FFF **Evening meal** by request **Credit Cards** no **Children** no **Disabled** yes **Pets** yes **Closed** never **Languages** English, Spanish **Proprietor** Christiane Bordes

Bouglon, S of Marmande

Domaine de Montfleuri

Set on a hillside with a pleasant garden, this strictly vegetarian household offers weekend workshops on pottery, relaxation or painting. The house is over 200 years old; Dominique has been here since 1991. Bedrooms are adequate: two have wheelchair access while baths and high chairs are ready for babies. The five-course evening meals are appetising with excellent desserts. Meat eaters can find restaurants in Bouglon. Swimming-pool.

Directions 15 km S of Marmande. Take D 933. Turn right at le Clavier. Drive through Bouglon on D 147. Well-signposted.

❖ 47250 Bouglon **Tel** 53 20 61 30 **Rooms** 4 **Prices** FF
Evening meal by request **Credit Cards** no **Children** yes
Disabled yes **Pets** no **Closed** never **Languages** English
Proprietor Dominique Barron

Brassac, NW of Moissac

La Marquise

The Dio family have farmed this land for more than half a century. Now they offer guests the best of both worlds: a working farm that is not too rural for city folk. Decorated and opened in 1992, the bedrooms in the stone farmhouse are rustic with exposed beams and the usual flowery fabrics. The big attraction is Michèle's cooking, which won a gold medal in 1991. She uses their own geese and ducks; her light pastry tart is a speciality.

Directions 35 km NW of Moissac. Take N 113 to Valence. Turn right on D 953 for Lauzette. Left on D 7 to Brassac. Signposted.

❖ Brassac, 82190 Bourg de Visa **Tel** 63 94 25 16 **Rooms** 4
Prices FF **Evening meal** by request **Credit Cards** no
Children yes **Disabled** no **Pets** yes **Closed** never
Languages English **Proprietors** Gilbert and Michèle Dio

Castelnau-de-M., NW of Bordeaux

Château du Foulon

A long, tree-lined drive leads to this well-maintained country house with parkland and lake. Many guests come here to see 'how the other half lives'. In the peach-coloured hall, there is a display of Bayeux porcelain; the green-walled dining-room, like other rooms, has fine antique furniture. The bedrooms and bathrooms are equally stylish and spotlessly clean. No *table d'hôte* is offered but there are many nearby restaurants.

Directions 28 km NW of Bordeaux. Take D1 to Castelnau. Château is just before village on left, well-signed.

❖ 33480 Castelnau-de-Médoc **Tel** 56 58 20 18 **Fax** 56 58 23 43 **Rooms** 5 **Prices** FFF **Evening meal** no **Credit Cards** no **Children** yes **Disabled** yes **Pets** no **Closed** Christmas, New Year **Languages** English **Proprietors** Vicomte and Vicomtesse J de Baritault du Carpia

Castex, S of Toulouse

Manzac D'En Bas

From London's Ritz Hotel to the Pyrenean foothills: that's the career change David Hopkins made in 1992. The former general manager applies the same standards of courtesy in the converted Ariège farmhouse, but informality is the rule for guests who walk, ski or just relax. Venetia, now the district nurse, bakes her whole-meal bread in an ancient oven as part of a 'modern' French break-fast. Already a popular weekend spot for folk from Toulouse.

Directions 65 km S of Toulouse. N 117; D 627 to Daumazan; D 19 to Castex; right after 2 km; after 600 m, house on left, up hill.

❖ 09350 Castex **Tel and Fax** 61 69 85 25 **Rooms** 3 **Prices** FF **Evening meal** by request **Credit Cards** no **Children** yes **Disabled** no **Pets** no **Closed** never **Languages** English, French **Proprietors** David and Venetia Hopkins

Clairac, SE of Tonneins

Le Caussinat

Rows of purple petunias and trees line the driveway, the gardens
are well-kept and fields stretch beyond. Once inside the large, tiled
hallway, this is a pretty, if old-fashioned, house with floral wallpaper, wood floors and thick rugs. The two sisters who live here
somehow manage to run the farm and its orchards, welcome
guests and cook for them. The bedroom furniture is heavy and
dark: big beds, cavernous wardrobes, upright chairs.
Directions 11 km SE of Tonneins. D 911 to Clairac. House is 2 km
further along D 666.

❖ 47320 Clairac **Tel** 53 84 22 11 **Rooms** 5 **Prices** FF
Evening meal by request **Credit Cards** no **Children** yes
Disabled no **Pets** no **Closed** never **Languages** some English,
Spanish **Proprietors** Gisèle and Aimé Massias

Esclottes, NW of Duras

Petito

When French housewives ask a retired Englishman for his recipes,
he must be doing something right. The carefully restored, 200-
year-old farmhouse is surrounded by plum orchards. The attractive main room has stone walls and high beams. Most guests 'live
outdoors' on the terrace by the swimming-pool. Dinner might
include tuna with red peppers, grilled figs with caramel sauce.
Value for money.
Directions 7 km NW of Duras. Take D 237; village signposted on
right. House well-signposted.

❖ Esclottes, 47120 Duras **Tel** 53 83 83 21 **Fax** 53 83 80 14
Rooms 3 **Prices** FF **Evening meal** yes **Credit Cards** no
Children yes **Disabled** no **Pets** yes **Closed** Oct to Easter
Languages English, Italian **Proprietor** Geoffrey Whitaker

Féas, SW of Oloron-Ste-Marie

Château de Bouès

This oblong château with towers at each end is 200 years old but looks quite modern. The high-ceilinged, renovated bedrooms are equally contemporary, which comes as a surprise after seeing the dining-room with its dark wooden ceiling, heavy furniture and hunting trophies on the wall. Everything is neat, tidy and practical; the owner is warm and helpful. The well-maintained grounds have a new swimming-pool, swings for the children. Trout-fishing.
Directions 8 km SW of Oloron-Ste-Marie. Take D 919. Château clearly signposted on left before Féas.

❖ 64570 Féas **Tel** 59 39 95 49 **Rooms** 4 **Prices** FFF
Evening meal no **Credit Cards** V **Children** yes **Disabled** no
Pets yes **Closed** Nov to March **Languages** English, Spanish
Proprietor Monique Dornon

Fourquevaux, SE of Toulouse

Château de Fourquevaux

More of a fortified manor house than a castle, this is also more of a hotel than a bed-and-breakfast. The Faux family have been decidedly business-like in their efforts to restore this square, severe, 16thC brick building in the heart of a small village. Overnight guests also benefit: tastefully decorated bedrooms with high-beamed ceilings, spacious enough for tables and chairs. A small restaurant at the castle gate provides evening meals.
Directions 18 km SE of Toulouse. Leave Toulouse on the D 2 towards Revel. The village is just off the main road on the left.

❖ 31450 Fourquevaux **Tel** 61 81 45 90 **Fax** 61 27 24 39 **Rooms** 6
Prices FFFF **Evening meal** no **Credit Cards** no **Children** yes
Disabled no **Pets** yes **Closed** never **Languages** English, Spanish
Proprietors Pierre and Corinne Faux

Gramat

Moulin de Fresquet

Gérard Ramelot, who is a painter, restored his former water-mill on the Alzou River skilfully and almost single-handedly. Bedrooms have a rural sophistication: original beams, tiled floors, pale floral bedspreads and tapestries on rough, painted walls. Light, modern bathrooms. Claude cooks everything herself, including pastries. Her five-course dinner, served communally at the big table, is excellent value. Delightful ambience.

Directions SW of Gramat. Take the N 140 towards Figeac. Turn left after 500 m. Mill is at end of track, past timber mill.

❖ 46500 Gramat **Tel** 65 38 70 60 **Rooms** 5 **Prices** FF
Evening meal by request **Credit Cards** no **Children** yes
Disabled yes **Pets** no **Closed** Nov to mid-March
Languages English **Proprietors** Gérard and Claude Ramelot

Haut-de-Bosdarros, S of Pau

Ferme Loutares

The lively owners, qualified in health and beauty treatments, run a spa as well as *chambres d'hôtes*. The remote setting is pretty, with gardens and a fine swimming-pool. The restored outbuildings of an old farm have new uses: the stables are the dining area; the barn, with beams and stone, are neat bedrooms. Evening meals have a diet menu plus regional favourites such as *poule au pot* and *confit de canard*. Ponies for children to ride.

Directions 30 km S of Pau. Take N 134; left at Rébénacq on D 936. D 388 for Haut-de-Bosdarros, small road.

❖ 64800 Haut-de-Bosdarros **Tel** 59 71 20 60 **Rooms** 4
Prices FFF **Evening meal** yes **Credit Cards** no **Children** yes
Disabled no **Pets** no **Closed** never **Languages** some Spanish,
English **Proprietors** Marie de Monteverde-Pucheu and
daughter Béatrice

Listrac-Médoc, NW of Bordeaux

Château Cap-Léon Veyrin

For five generations the Meyre family have lived in this unpretentious, square yellow house. They are known as wine makers and each bedroom is named after a grape variety such as Merlot or Malbec. All are centrally heated and well-decorated with floral wallpapers, tiled floors, rugs, and antiques. Mattresses are firm. Tapestries decorate the dining-room where dinner is served at a long table. Excellent value for money.

Directions 34 km NW of Bordeaux. Take D1 via Castelnau-de-Médoc on to Listrac. Well-signposted beyond village.

❖ Donissan, 33480 Listrac-Médoc **Tel** 56 58 07 28
Fax 56 58 07 50 **Rooms** 5 **Prices** FF **Evening meal** by request
Credit Cards no **Children** yes **Disabled** no **Pets** no
Closed mid-Dec to mid-Jan **Languages** English, Spanish
Proprietors M and Mme Alain Meyre

Monclar d'A., NW of Villeneuve-sur-Lot

La Seiglal

This looks grand, with parkland stretching in all directions. Inside, burgundy fabric paper covers the walls, wood floors shine. In the dining-room, the long table is covered with a lace cloth and candelabras; in the library, the stone fireplace has a handsome carved mantel. A stone staircase leads from the Games Room (once the entrance hall) to the bedrooms. At 8 pm the castle bell announces dinner.

Directions 5 km NW of Villeneuve-sur-Lot. Take D 911; D 667 at Ste-Livrade, D 113 to Monclar. House 2 km from village.

❖ 47380 Monclar d'Agenais **Tel** 53 41 81 30 **Fax** 53 41 85 10
Rooms 5 **Prices** FFF-FFFF **Evening meal** by request
Credit Cards no **Children** yes **Disabled** no **Pets** no **Closed** never
Languages French only **Proprietors** Christian and Henriette Decourty

Monflanquin

Domaine de Roquefère

Mother and son have worked hard to convert buildings on their working farm into a bed-and-breakfast and value-for-money *ferme auberge*. 'Contemporary rustic' is how one guest described bedrooms with patterned bedspreads and rugs on tiled floors. Each has a terrace and private bath. Breakfast is *copieux*: muffins, cereals, fresh fruit, eggs. The swimming-pool is for guests only. Open since 1992, we give this a high rating.

Directions 2 km NW of Monflanquin. Take D 676 towards Villeréal. Roquefère is on left, signposted.

❖ 47150 Monflanquin **Tel** 53 36 43 74 **Rooms** 6 **Prices** FF
Evening meal by request **Credit Cards** no **Children** yes
Disabled no **Pets** yes **Closed** never: telephone
Languages English, Italian, Spanish, Portuguese
Proprietors Mme Semelier and son Francis

Monflanquin

L'Ormeraie

The owner's good taste shows in this 300-year-old manor house flanked by tall oaks, and with a park, rose garden and heated swimming-pool. His library has 3,000 books; antiques, paintings and Oriental rugs abound. Centrally heated bedrooms vary from turn-of-the-century to modern; bathrooms have heated rails. The Grand Atelier has stone walls, a pine ceiling and a bed up spiral stairs. Evening meals no longer served; plenty of local restaurants.

Directions 8 km NE of Monflanquin. Take D 272 to Laussou, not Paulhiac. Turn right to Bonnenouvelle; house on right.

❖ Paulhiac, 47150 Monflanquin **Tel** 53 36 45 96
Fax 53 36 47 73 **Rooms** 6 **Prices** FFF **Evening meal** no
Credit Cards MC V **Children** yes **Disabled** yes **Pets** yes
Closed mid-Nov to mid-April **Languages** English, Spanish
Proprietor Michel de l'Ormeraie

Monségur, SW of Duras

Château de la Bûche

The owners went from computers to co-operatives when they left Paris in 1991 to renovate an 18thC château. They send the grapes from their next-door vineyard to the co-op and guests can taste the result with the well-priced evening meal. Dominique prepares local dishes such as *salade landaise* and *porc aux pruneaux*. The bedrooms are newly decorated but plain with heavy old furniture. One has wheelchair access.

Directions 9 km SW of Duras. Take D 668. House is on right on entering Monségur.

❖ 10 avenue de la Porte des Tours, 33580 Monségur
Tel 56 61 80 22 **Rooms** 5 **Prices** FF **Evening meal** obligatory
Credit Cards no **Children** yes **Disabled** yes **Pets** no
Closed never **Languages** English **Proprietors** M and Mme Ledru

Montferrand-du-Périgord, SE of Bergerac

La Rivière

This well-maintained, well-organised farm produces sheep, ducks and cereals and is run by an enthusiastic, helpful family. Evening meals are highly rated. Sylvie, who focuses on regional dishes, runs cookery courses in the winter. A separate entrance leads to bedrooms which have beige carpets, cream bedspreads, pine ceilings, firm mattresses, electric heating, practical bathrooms. The swimming-pool overlooks the farm.

Directions 37 km SE of Bergerac. D 660 E along Dordogne; cross at Port-de-Couze. D 26 to Montferrand; farm past town.

❖ 24440 Montferrand-du-Périgord **Tel** 53 63 25 25 **Rooms** 3
Prices FF **Evening meal** by request **Credit Cards** no
Children yes **Disabled** no **Pets** yes **Closed** never
Languages some English, Spanish **Proprietor** Sylvie Barriat-Sinico

Montpezat-de-Quercy, S of Cahors

Le Barry

Built into the medieval ramparts, this house was renovated in 1992. Despite the swimming-pool in the garden, the sense of history has been preserved. Books and music fill the light sitting-room; prints, sketches, portraits and photos line the walls. The bedrooms and bathrooms are comfortable and practical 'with no frills'; one has wheelchair access and the owners are willing to help. They join guests for the well-priced dinner. First-class.

Directions 25 km S of Cahors. Take N 20, then D 20 W to main square of village. Right from Mairie, then left. 300 m on right.

❖ Faubourg St-Roch, 82270 Montpezat-de-Quercy
Tel 63 02 05 50 **Fax** 63 02 03 07 **Rooms** 5 **Prices** FFF
Evening meal by request **Credit Cards** no **Children** yes
Disabled yes **Pets** yes **Closed** Jan, Feb **Languages** English,
German, Italian, some Spanish **Proprietors** Francis Bankes,
Lothar Jaross

Moustier, NE of Marmande

La Croix de Moustier

Our inspector enjoyed staying on this working farm, where 'bedrooms are basic but clean and comfortable'. On a hot afternoon, the swimming-pool was especially welcome with extra towels ready in the bedroom. The owner's wife, a good cook, prepares kidneys with prunes, duck, and cakes. She even brews an aperitif of sweet wine, orange juice and chicory. Breakfast was disappointing, but this still offers value for money.

Directions 32 km NE of Marmande. Take D 933 to Miramont; turn left on D 668 to Moustier. Well-signposted.

❖ Moustier, 47800, Miramont de Guyenne **Tel** 53 20 21 87
Rooms 5 **Prices** FF **Evening meal** by request **Credit Cards** no
Children yes **Disabled** yes **Pets** yes **Closed** never
Languages English **Proprietors** Nicole and Jean-Claude Palu

Nègrepelisse, NE of Montauban

Les Brunis

This restored 150-year-old farmhouse with its pink walls and red tiles overlooks a swimming-pool. Each bedroom has its own entrance: one has wooden steps up to a separate children's room; another has a bathroom with sunken bath. 'I haven't seen better in a three star hotel,' decided our inspector. Véronique prepares Tarn specialities such as asparagus and goats' cheese quiche but she will also cook to guests' wishes.

Directions 30 km NE of Montauban. Take D 115 to Nègrepelisse. Left on D 958 for Montricoux. Sign on right.

❖ 82800 Nègrepelisse **Tel** 63 67 24 08 **Rooms** 5 **Prices** FF
Evening meal by request **Credit Cards** no **Children** yes
Disabled yes **Pets** yes **Closed** never **Languages** English
Proprietors Johnny and Véronique Antony

Paleyrac, SE of Périgueux

Les Farguettes

The owner writes for the theatre, his Swiss wife is a poet. She decorated this 300-year-old stone house with style, using Italian fabrics for the curtains and bedspreads in the particularly comfortable carpeted bedrooms. The sitting-room has a television and there are plans to 'create a proper library'. Meals, eaten family-style at a long table, include local and Mediterranean dishes. Swimming-pool, garden, horses at nearby ranch.

Directions 50 km SE of Périgueux. Take D 710 to le Bugue; D 31e to le Buisson, then D 25 to Paleyrac. Signposted.

❖ Paleyrac, 24480 Le Buisson **Tel** 53 23 48 23 **Rooms** 3
Prices FFF **Evening meal** by request **Credit Cards** no
Children yes **Disabled** no **Pets** yes **Closed** never; telephone in
winter **Languages** English, German, Spanish
Proprietors Françoise and Claude de Torrenté

Prudhomat, SW of Bretenoux

Domaine de Vayssières

Outward appearances are deceptive: a broken gate, a half-built swimming-pool; yet the creeper-clad stone house is charming, with central heating throughout. Bedrooms have old-fashioned furniture but new mattresses and were redecorated recently. One, in a separate building, has wheelchair access. The hosts are friendly and amusing; ask about the battles with the builders over the swimming-pool. Dinner, bed-and-breakfast only: excellent value.

Directions 3 km SW of Bretenoux. Take D 14 along Dordogne River to village; well-signposted.

❖ 46130 Prudhomat **Tel** 65 38 50 22 **Rooms** 6 **Prices** FF
Evening meal included **Credit Cards** no **Children** yes
Disabled yes **Pets** yes **Closed** never **Languages** French only
Proprietors Marie-José and Jean de la Barrière

St-Emilion

Château Millaud-Montlabert

'A pleasure to meet this energetic, enthusiastic hostess,' whose renovated farmhouse has been in the family for 200 years. A separate entrance leads to carpeted bedrooms with modern furniture and bedspreads made by the owner. Guests may use the refrigerator, cooker and washing machine; a television is in the sitting-room. Meals are recommended, especially the chocolate gâteau. Central heating. Grand Cru wines made and sold here.

Directions 3 km NW of St-Emilion. Take D 243; right on D 245 for Pomerol. Château 300 m.

❖ 33330 St-Emilion **Tel** 57 24 71 85 **Fax** 57 24 62 78 **Rooms** 5
Prices FF **Evening meal** by request **Credit Cards** no
Children yes **Disabled** no **Pets** no **Closed** Jan **Languages** some
English, Spanish **Proprietors** Jacqueline and Claude Brieux

St-Ferme, NW of Duras

Château du Parc

In the heart of the Entre Deux Mers vineyards, this 18thC château once housed the abbot of St Ferme. Today, the Lalandes have gone unashamedly up market: 'the sort of decoration and furniture you see in glossy magazines,' says one guest, 'with flowers throughout.' Up the stone staircase are bedrooms with embroidered linens. The wood floors are attractively stencilled in blue by Madame Lalande who also made the curtains and bedcovers.

Directions 10 km NW of Duras. Take D 668 SW to Monségur. Go 10 km N on D 16 to St-Ferme. Well-signposted.

❖ 33580 St-Ferme **Tel** 56 61 69 18 **Fax** 56 61 69 23 **Rooms** 5
Prices FFFF **Evening meal** by request **Credit Cards** AE DC MC
V **Children** no **Disabled** yes **Pets** yes **Closed** never
Languages English **Proprietors** Bertrand and Sophie Lalande

St-Julien-le-Vendômois, S of Limoges

Domaine de la Roche

In one of France's most rural areas, the Castellaccis produce *foie gras* and *magret de canard* on their farm. Since 1991, the Marquise has cooked traditional dishes such as *blanquette de veau*. Reports are enthusiastic for desserts. Three rustic bedrooms were opened in 1992 but 'there's no farm smell' according to one guest. In winter, the *auberge* is closed so evening meals are rarely available. Check ahead of time.

Directions 58 km S of Limoges. D 704 to St-Yrieix; D 126 via Quinsac for Arnac-Pompadour; house 3 km after St-Julien.

❖ 19210 St-Julien-le-Vendômois **Tel** 55 98 72 87 **Fax** 55 73 68 41
Rooms 3 **Prices** FF **Evening meal** by request **Credit Cards** no
Children yes **Disabled** no **Pets** yes **Closed** never
Languages English, Italian **Proprietor** Marquise Castellacci

St-Martin-de-Laye, N of Libourne

Gaudart

Although difficult to find, our inspectors were attracted by the rural isolation, the prices and the attentiveness of the hosts. The farmhouse, a family home for many years, was modernised in the mid-1980s, so rooms are practical rather than atmospheric. Bedrooms have independent access and electric heating. The hosts' own wine is offered but note that dinner is not served in July and August. The nearest restaurant is 5 km.

Directions 16 km N of Libourne. Take D 910; then D 22 via St-Denis, through Bonzac. Farm is signposted up lane on right.

❖ 33910 St-Martin-de-Laye **Tel** 57 49 41 37 **Rooms** 3 **Prices** FFF
Evening meal by request **Credit Cards** no **Children** yes
Disabled no **Pets** no **Closed** Nov to March **Languages** French
only **Proprietors** Josette and Michel Garret

Sames, SW of Peyrehorade

Le Lanot

Liliane 'who speaks English, of course' modernized this 200-year-old farmhouse in 1990, and now enjoys rural life with her dogs. There is a pond in the well-tended garden; breakfast is served in the plant-filled conservatory. Candle-lit dinner, which is quite expensive, might include salad, half a duck, vegetables, local goats' cheese and gâteaus. The beamed bedrooms have old-fashioned furniture; one, in the attic, can sleep a family of five.

Directions 6 km SW of Peyrehorade. Take D 23 south of the river. Follow signs in Sames.

❖ 64520 Sames **Tel** 59 56 01 84 **Rooms** 3 **Prices** FF
Evening meal by request **Credit Cards** AE V **Children** yes
Disabled yes **Pets** yes **Closed** never; check in winter
Languages English, some Spanish **Proprietor** Liliane Mickelson

Sare, SE of St-Jean-de-Luz

Olhabidea

The Pyrenees are a dramatic backdrop for a 16thC half-timbered house with wooden balconies. The hall is galleried, an inglenook fireplace dominates the sitting-room. Beams and dark wood furniture stand out against white walls. The stylish bedrooms are different shapes and sizes: one has a green carpet with tartan bedspread and curtains; another is in blue and white. The proud owner wants guests to enjoy her home. Five restaurants nearby.
Directions 15 km SE of St-Jean-de-Luz. Take D 918 to St-Pée; then D 3, D 4 for Sare. House on left, opposite chapel. No signs.

❖ 64310 Sare **Tel** 59 54 21 85 **Rooms** 4 **Prices** FFF
Evening meal no **Credit Cards** no **Children** over 12 **Disabled** no
Pets no **Closed** Nov to March **Languages** English, Spanish
Proprietor Anne-Marie Fagoaga

Sourzac-Mussidan, SW of Périgueux

Le Chaufourg

'The bathrooms are truly exceptional' according to one guest, impressed by the sheer style of this 17thC house in the Isle Valley. Luxurious and expensive, there is not a painting or antique out of place. The owner, a well-known photographer, has definite tastes: some may find the furnishings too fussy, but the quality can't be faulted. Television and telephones are in bedrooms, a swimming-pool is in the garden.
Directions 35 km SW of Périgueux. Take N 89; house is on right just before Sourzac.

❖ 24400 Sourzac-Mussidan **Tel** 53 81 01 56 **Fax** 53 82 94 87
Rooms 7 **Prices** FFFF **Evening meal** by request **Credit Cards** MC
V **Children** no **Disabled** no **Pets** no **Closed** never
Languages English **Proprietor** Georges Dambier

Tourtoirac, E of Périgueux

Le Moulin de la Crouzille

The British owners converted a riverside mill as a holiday home but now live here all year. Although there is an English ambience with some English antiques, the cooking is French. Diana prepares *magret de canard* and rabbit, plus home-grown vegetables. Wine from St-Emilion is included in the price. The bedrooms get the afternoon sun. A swimming-pool has just been built. Guests find the hosts' tourist tips especially helpful.

Directions 35 km E of Périgueux. D 5 along Auvezère valley; 2 km after Tourtoirac, left to La Crouzille. First on right after bridge.

❖ Tourtoirac, 24390 Hautefort **Tel** 53 51 11 94 **Rooms** 2
Prices FF **Evening meal** yes **Credit Cards** no **Children** yes
Disabled no **Pets** no **Closed** never **Languages** English
Proprietors John and Diana Armitage

Turenne, SE of Brive

La Maison des Chanoines

This is a serious restaurant; yet its three bedrooms, limited size and personal touch match our requirements. The dining-room, bar and breakfast-room are in a creeper-clad, 400-year-old stone house. The high-quality bedrooms have a separate entrance. Two are lively and modern, with small sitting-rooms and yellow, white and green spring colours. Bathrooms have white tiles with a golfing motif. The third bedroom sleeps five. Some antiques.

Directions 16 km SE of Brive. Take D 38, then D 8 to Turenne. In middle of village.

❖ route du Château, Le Bourg, 19500 Turenne **Tel** 55 85 93 43
Rooms 3 **Prices** FFF **Evening meal** not Tues, Weds
Credit Cards MC V **Children** yes **Disabled** no **Pets** yes
Closed mid-Nov to mid-Feb **Languages** English
Proprietors Claude and Chantal Cheyroux

Varilhes, N of Foix

Las Rives

'Guests seem to be young and active' reported our inspectors who were impressed by the large, family home by the Ariège River. 'It offers more than some first-class hotels': a clay tennis-court, a fine swimming-pool, bicycles and horses. The owners, keen cyclists, have mapped routes in the Pyrenean foothills. Bedrooms are carpeted, clean and simple. Gardens and grounds are well-maintained with slides and table tennis for children.

Directions 10 km N of Foix. Take N 20 to Varilhes. Follow directions to Rieux, across bridge; turn left and follow signs.

❖ 09120 Varilhes **Tel** 61 60 73 42 **Rooms** 5 **Prices** FF
Evening meal no **Credit Cards** no **Children** yes **Disabled** no
Pets no **Closed** never **Languages** English, Spanish
Proprietors M and Mme Jean Baudeigne

Villeneuve-sur-Lot

Les Huguets

Ward Poppe-Notteboom farms the valley, growing organic vegetables and vines; he also has nine horses and is a keen musician. His wife, Gerda, is a capable cook and, unusually, offers lunch as well as dinner. The sitting-room doubles as a dining room in inclement weather. In the beamed bedrooms, floors are carpeted and mosquito nets hang from the ceilings. The basement houses a pine-panelled exercise room and sauna.

Directions Just S of Villeneuve. Take N 21 for Agen. Look for signposts just after first roundabout. First road on left.

❖ 47300 Villeneuve-sur-Lot **Tel** 53 70 49 34 **Rooms** 5 **Prices** FFF
Evening meal and lunch by request **Credit Cards** no
Children yes **Disabled** yes **Pets** no **Closed** never
Languages English, Dutch **Proprietors** Ward and Gerda
Poppe-Notteboom

➡ *More on page 184*

Bellegarde, E of Albi

La Borie Neuve

Alongside the renovated 16thC farmhouse, Madame Richard opened a separate building in 1993. The four bedrooms, with cork-tiled floors, modern furniture, and plain bathrooms, have a terrace and views over the garden and Tarn Valley. The main house has five more modernized bedrooms above the dining-room, with its beige ceramic tiles and sandy, plastered walls. Madame cooks, then joins her guests at the long, modern table.

Directions 12 km E of Albi. Take D 999 for Millau. After Foncouverte, first right to Bellegarde. House is first on left.

❖ 81430 Bellegarde **Tel** 63 55 33 64 **Rooms** 9 **Prices** FF **Evening meal** by request **Credit Cards** no **Children** yes **Disabled** yes **Pets** yes **Closed** never **Languages** English, Spanish **Proprietor** Mme Jacqueline Richard

Cahuzac-sur-Vère, N of Gaillac

Place de l'Eglise

This old village house, festooned with ivy, has a large lemon tree growing in a wooden cask outside. Inside the tiled hall, are a pair of forge bellows and a narrow, spiral wooden staircase. M Miraille loves to talk about his hobby, bee keeping. His wife, Claudine, is well-known in the area for her simple, traditional dishes. So much so, she occasionally accommodates the overflow from two local restaurants. Clean, fresh bedrooms.

Directions Cahuzac is 11 km N of Gaillac. From Gaillac, take D 992. Place de l'Eglise is in middle of village, by church.

❖ Place de l'Eglise, 81480 Cahuzac-sur-Vère **Tel** 63 33 91 53 **Rooms** 4 **Prices** FF **Evening meal** by request **Credit Cards** no **Children** yes **Disabled** yes **Pets** no **Closed** never **Languages** some Spanish **Proprietors** Miraille family

Cambounet-s/l-Sor, SW of Castres

Château de la Serre

The owners spent 35 years in Africa before returning home in 1992 and opening the castle, which has been in Madame's family since the French Revolution. Only essential modernisation has been carried out: on bathrooms, curtains, bedspreads. Otherwise antiques, family portraits and African memorabilia help to fill the large rooms. Dried flowers and plants abound. The atmosphere is comfortable, the look is pleasantly eclectic.

Directions 13 km SW of Castres. Take N 126. After 11 km, turn right for Cambounet on D 14. Follow signs in village.

❖ 81580 Cambounet-sur-le-Sor **Tel** 63 71 75 73 **Fax** 63 71 76 06 **Rooms** 3 **Prices** FFFF **Evening meal** by request **Credit Cards** No **Children** yes **Disabled** no **Pets** yes **Closed** Oct to April **Languages** some English, Italian, Spanish **Proprietors** Chantal and Guy Berthoumieux

Gaillac

8 place St-Michel

The 17thC townhouse is in the medieval heart of Gaillac, facing the Abbaye. Imposing wooden double doors open off the street. A massive stone staircase leads to the upper levels. Persian rugs cover the stone and oak floors; antiques and leather sofas abound; the dining-room has a carved stone fireplace. Breakfast on the terrace offers views over the Abbaye, the Tarn and old rooftops. Bedrooms are large, airy and very comfortable.

Directions The place St-Michel is in front of the Abbaye St-Michel. In the one-way system, follow signs for the Abbaye.

❖ 8 place St-Michel, 81600 Gaillac **Tel** 63 57 61 48 **Fax** 63 41 06 56 **Rooms** 6 **Prices** FF **Evening meal** by request **Credit Cards** no **Children** yes **Disabled** no **Pets** yes **Closed** never **Languages** English **Proprietors** Lucile and Jean-Luc Pinon

Lempaut, SW of Castres

La Bousquétarié

With a swimming-pool, tennis-court, bikes and table tennis, there is plenty to do here. Set in a park, the *manoir*-château is full of Empire furniture and the family's grown-up children are often around, creating a warm ambience. Breakfast is in the kitchen, aperitifs in the garden. A dinner of asparagus, grilled salmon and courgettes *au gratin* was praised by a guest who stayed in 'granny's bedroom' with its huge marble-floored bathroom.

Directions 18 km SW of Castres. Take N126 to Soual, then D622 towards Revel. Follow signs.

❖ 81700 Lempaut **Tel** 63 75 51 09 **Rooms** 3 **Prices** FFF
Evening meal by request **Credit Cards** no **Children** yes
Disabled no **Pets** yes **Closed** never **Languages** English
Proprietors Charles and Monique Sallier

Lempaut, SW of Castres

La Rode

Breakfast is served in the cloistered courtyard of this former 16thC convent. Guests use a large room with table tennis and an adjoining kitchen for preparing picnics or simple meals (restaurants are nearby). Up the wide stone stairs, old-fashioned bedrooms with stained glass windows are spotlessly clean. Family heirlooms abound: sketches, pictures, an old clock. A little down-at-heel, perhaps, but ideal for families on a budget. Deep in the country.

Directions 18 km SW of Castres. Take N 126 to Soual, then D 622 towards Revel. Look for signs on right.

❖ 81700 Lempaut **Tel and Fax** 63 75 51 07 **Rooms** 3 **Prices** FF
Evening meal no **Credit Cards** no **Children** yes **Disabled** no
Pets yes **Closed** Nov to March **Languages** English
Proprietors M and Mme Gaétan de Falguerolles

Lempaut, SW of Castres

Villa Les Pins

It is a surprise to find a turn-of-the-century Italian villa at the end of the tree-lined avenue. Family heirlooms fill the large, elegant rooms and hallways with their polished wood floors. Breakfast and dinner are served outdoors on the terrace, in the panelled kitchen, or grey and yellow dining-room. The bedrooms are comfortable, and if there is a slightly faded look, guests say it is 'relaxing and informal when you're on holiday'.

Directions 18 km SW of Castres. N126 to Soval, D622 for Revel, through Lempaut for Blan; on left before churchyard.

❖ 81700 Lempaut **Tel** 63 75 51 01 **Rooms** 5 **Prices** FF
Evening meal by request **Credit Cards** no **Children** yes
Disabled no **Pets** no **Closed** Nov to March **Languages** English
Proprietor Marie-Paule Delbreil

Molezon, SE of Florac

Château de la Rouvière

Since 1991, the Matthews have lived in this fortified 16thC Cévennes house, set in a spectacular mountain valley. Jean specializes in a wide variety of vegetarian dishes, using the rich supply of Mediterranean fruits and vegetables, but 'guests can have meat dishes if they ask in advance'. Three bedrooms in the square tower, all with lovely views, are popular with hikers in spring and autumn since several national trails are nearby.

Directions 25 km SE of Florac. Take D 983 via St-Laurent, Barres-des-Cévennes; house is where mountain road meets valley.

❖ Molezon, 48110 Ste-Croix-Vallée-Française **Tel** 66 45 06 19
Rooms 5 **Prices** FF **Evening meal** yes **Credit Cards** no
Children yes **Disabled** no **Pets** no **Closed** never
Languages English **Proprietors** Tony and Jean Matthews

Domaine des Juliannes

Here is France's first Gîte Panda, with nature trails for observing the wildlife of this unspoiled region, but people also come for the horses. Qualified instructors take beginners and experts on trails and also teach show-jumping. Some guests, however, just relax by the swimming-pool. Marc prepares regional dishes such as *cassoulet*, Claudine's speciality is chocolate desserts. Bedrooms, in a separate, renovated stone building, are rustic but comfortable.
Directions 38 km E of Albi. Take D 999. Turn right on D 86 before Alban; then left D 53 to Paulinet. Follow signs.

❖ Paulinet, 81250 Alban **Tel** 63 55 94 38 **Rooms** 6 **Prices** FFF **Evening meal** by request **Credit Cards** V **Children** yes **Disabled** no **Pets** yes **Closed** Nov to Feb **Languages** English **Proprietors** Marc and Claudine Choucavy

Le Merlet

The Montagne du Bougès is a landmark in the rugged country-side favoured by hikers. Some stop for the night here *en route*; more and more use the Galzins as a base, since the evening meals are remarkable value: vegetable soup, lamb with aubergines, goat cheeses, blueberry tart: all local or home-made. The owners have slowly renovated two granite houses with slate roofs. Bedrooms are newly decorated, comfortable and rustic. Well worth finding.
Directions 27 km E of Florac. D 998 to le Pont-de-Montvert; 5 km on left, steep road climbs to Le Merlet and Felgerolles.

❖ 48220 Le Pont-de-Montvert **Tel** 66 45 82 92 **Rooms** 5 **Prices** FF **Evening meal** yes **Credit Cards** no **Children** yes **Disabled** no **Pets** no **Closed** never **Languages** French only **Proprietors** M and Mme Philippe Galzin

Le Plaix

Even though our inspectors arrived, incognito, at 8.30 pm, they were welcomed warmly and joined the Raucaz family for a satisfying country dinner by the inglenook fireplace. Meat and vegetables come from the farm and Claire makes her own jams. The plain bedrooms, overlooking farmland, are reached by a stone staircase in the square tower.

Directions 35 km S of Nevers. Take N 7 for Moulins. Exit at St-Pierre-le-Moutier. Go SW on D 978a to Le Veurdre. Go left 1.5 km on D 13; turn right on D 234. House signposted, 3 km on right.

❖ 03320 Pouzy-Mésangy **Tel** 70 66 24 06 **Fax** 70 66 25 82
Rooms 5 **Prices** FF **Evening meal** by request **Credit Cards** V
Children yes **Disabled** no **Pets** yes **Closed** never
Languages some English, Italian **Proprietors** Claire and Georges Raucaz

Laval

This farm has been in the Roques family since 1872. The farmhouse has high, beamed ceilings, oak floors and heavy furniture. One vast room is both kitchen and dining-room with long table, grandfather clock, TV and large fireplace. Madame Roques prepares local specialities such as casseroles and makes her own jams. In fine weather, both breakfast and dinner are served on the terrace with its pink petunias, red geraniums and roses.

Directions 23 km NW of Gaillac. Follow D 964 past Castelnau. Laval is on the left before Puycelsi.

❖ Puycelsi, 81140 Castelnau-de-Montmirail **Tel** 63 33 11 07
Rooms 3 **Prices** FF **Evening meal** by request **Credit Cards** no
Children yes **Disabled** no **Pets** yes **Closed** never
Languages some English **Proprietors** Roques family

St-Frézal-de-Ventalon, NW of Alès

Le Viala

The hosts are avid hikers who bought an old ruin some 15 years ago and made it into a snug home. Jean, a qualified guide, is passionate about local history, and takes guests hiking. Lili uses seasonal produce, such as chestnuts and mushrooms in the autumn, to make 'refined rustic dishes'. Ringed by wooded mountains, the views from the plain rooms with Cévenol furniture are tranquil. Remote, hard to find so get directions locally.

Directions 50 km NW of Alès. N 106 along Gardon valley; D 29 to St-Frézal-de-Ventalon. House is below village in valley.

❖ 48240 St-Frézal-de-Ventalon **Tel** 66 45 54 08 **Rooms** 5
Prices FF **Evening meal** yes **Credit Cards** no **Children** yes
Disabled no **Pets** no **Closed** mid-Nov to Easter
Languages French only **Proprietors** Jean and Lili Demolder

St-Gerand-le-Puy, S of Varennes s/ Allier

Demeure des Payratons

This lovely 18thC mansion comes as a surprise. 'This has all the quality of a good hotel,' reports our inspector. A piano and harp sit in the elegant, pale green and gold sitting-room with its large wall mirrors. Overlooking the gardens, the bedrooms are up one floor, in delicate colours such as pale blue, gold or pink with matching bedspreads. Although Madame Poulet only opened in 1992, her elegant regional dishes already have a reputation.

Directions 10 km SE of Varennes-sur-Allier. Leave Varennes on N 7. Les Payratons is on right, just before St-Gerand-le-Puy.

❖ 03150 St-Gerand-le-Puy **Tel** 70 99 82 44 **Rooms** 4
Prices FF-FFF **Evening meal** by request **Credit Cards** AE MC V
Children yes **Disabled** no **Pets** yes **Closed** never
Languages Spanish **Proprietor** Madame Christiane Poulet

Domaine des Dômes

At this ranch-style farm, Gisèle Guillitte breeds American quarter horses and Appaloosas. The paddocks, stables and gardens are kept neat; children ride ponies or in a donkey cart. Bernard has run the bed-and-breakfast since 1992. In a modernised barn, separate from the owner's house, the bedrooms each have a theme: American, Greek, Japanese and African. His cooking is highly praised. Barbecues in summer.

Directions 20 km SE of Moulins. Take D 12 past airport. Left on E 62. Thiel is 6 km on right. Domaine well-signposted.

❖ 03230 Thiel-sur-Acolin **Tel and Fax** 70 42 54 28 **Rooms** 4
Prices FF **Evening meal** by request **Credit Cards** no
Children yes **Disabled** yes **Pets** yes **Closed** never
Languages English, Greek **Proprietors** Gisèle and Bernard
Guillitte

Le Cloître

In 1992, the Souvilles changed careers and bought this 15thC house in the shadow of the castle walls, with yellow roses by the blue front door. They kept *le jus*, the spirit of the building, with themed bedrooms: Louis XIII, Louis XVI and a suite with an orange floral canopy bed. The bathrooms are functional. Guests borrow the three bikes to explore local villages with the owner. Hunters come in autumn. Restaurant 50 m.

Directions 30 km S of Moulins. Take N 9, D 18. House on square in village.

❖ place de la Fontaine, 03500 Verneuil-en-Bourbonnais
Tel 70 45 47 58 **Rooms** 3 **Prices** FFF **Evening meal** no
Credit Cards no **Children** yes **Disabled** no **Pets** yes
Closed never; telephone in winter **Languages** some English,
German **Proprietors** Marie-Christiane and Pierre Souville

➡ *More on page 190*

Antibes

Le Bosquet

A few minutes from the Cap d'Antibes beaches, this 18thC house is an economical way to join the jet-set. The elegance and peace has changed little since writer Guy de Maupassant wintered here more than a century ago. The bedrooms (Blue, Yellow and Sea-urchins) echo yesteryear, with marble fireplaces, unusual head-boards and sofas. Dinner is served once a week to help guests to meet each other. Young owners, with children; opened in 1993.

Directions Between Juan-les-Pins and Antibes on the chemin des Sables.

❖ 14 chemin des Sables, avenue du Bosquet, 06600 Antibes
Tel 93 67 32 29 **Rooms** 3 **Prices** FFF **Evening meal** once a week
Credit Cards no **Children** yes **Disabled** no **Pets** yes
Closed never **Languages** some English **Proprietors** Sylvie and Christian Aussel

Aramon, SW of Avignon

Le Rocher Pointu

Hidden in the rocky hills, the poppy-lined twisting driveway leads eventually to a typical Provençal villa with white walls, beams and dried flowers: just enough decoration to be attractive, not over-whelming. Breakfast, with the addition of ham, eggs and cheese, is 'more like brunch'. Guests use the barbecue, kitchenette, washing machine and swimming-pool. Some sunbathe nude; prudes are welcome to cover up. Panoramic views.

Directions 12 km SW of Avignon. Take D2; then sharp right at Sanofi on D 126; left after 2.3 km to house.

❖ Plan de Dève, 30390 Aramon **Tel** 66 57 41 87
Fax 66 57 01 77 **Rooms** 4 **Prices** FFF **Evening meal** no
Credit Cards no **Children** yes **Disabled** yes **Pets** no **Closed** never
Languages English **Proprietors** André and Annie Malek

Argelès-sur-Mer, SE of Perpignan

Mas Reste

Not far from the sea and the Spanish border, Lucien Bes has modernised an old Catalan *mas*, or stone farmhouse. Some may feel that the minibars and televisons make bedrooms too hotel-like, but the air-conditioning is a plus in July and August. Bedrooms are named after a jewel: Emeraude, Saphir, Turquoise. Bathrooms have marble fittings. The swimming-pool plus laundrette make this particularly attractive for families. Fair value.
Directions 22 km SE of Perpignan. Take N 114. The house is on edge of Argelès-sur-Mer.

❖ chemin du Roua, 66700 Argelès-sur-Mer **Tel** 68 81 42 88 **Fax** 68 81 67 66 **Rooms** 6 **Prices** FFF **Evening meal** by request **Credit Cards** V **Children** yes **Disabled** no **Pets** no **Closed** never **Languages** English, Spanish, Italian **Proprietor** Lucien Bes

Asperjoc, N of Vals-les-Bains

Domaine de Combelle

Just outside the village by the river, this former silk merchant's house looks cold from the outside but the bedrooms are lovingly furnished. One, in '19thC English style', has wine-red carpeting, a grey marble fireplace, folding dressing screen, a double bed in an alcove and views into a chestnut tree outside. The vast 'Louis XVI' room has a sofa and armchairs; the '1930s-1940s' room has a (fake) fur bedspread. All the bathrooms are attractive.
Directions 1.5 km N of Vals-les-Bains. Take D 578 towards Antraigues. After 1.5 km turn left over bridge.

❖ Asperjoc, 07600 Vals-les-Bains **Tel** 75 37 62 77 **Rooms** 4 **Prices** FFF **Evening meal** no **Credit Cards** no **Children** yes **Disabled** no **Pets** yes **Closed** never **Languages** English **Proprietors** Christian and Caroline Reale-Mocquet

Bagnols-en-Forêt, N of Fréjus

Villa Arcadie

On the edge of a small cultivated plain, the modern, pink ranch-style, Provençal bungalow is set in pines. The swimming-pool is very much the focal point of what feels like a small hotel. Bedrooms are reached via the terrace and have fitted wardrobes, new carpets and furniture which is 'three-star hotel quality'. Multi-channel televisions can be hired. The Rollets used to run a restaurant and offer attractive meals, including lunch by the pool.

Directions 18 km N of Fréjus. Take D 4. Before Bagnols, follow signs for Chapelle St-Denis on left. House is 3 km past chapel.

❖ chemin de St-Denis, 83600 Bagnols-en-Forêt **Tel** 94 40 68 36
Fax 94 40 30 87 **Rooms** 6 **Prices** FFF **Evening meal** by request
Credit Cards no **Children** yes **Disabled** no **Pets** no
Closed never; telephone in winter **Languages** French only
Proprietors M and Mme Alain Rollet

Bauduen, S of Moustiers

Domaine de Majastre

The Ste-Croix lake and Verdon Gorge are perennial attractions, so this is a popular place. Perhaps that accounts for the 'small hotel' rather than 'bed-and-breakfast' ambience. Bedrooms are sophisticated, if old-fashioned; some have curtained alcoves for beds. Provençal favourites such as *pistou* and *pâté en croûte* are served in the small, somewhat cramped guests' dining-room. As well as a swimming-pool, the family has its own chapel with bold murals.

Directions 15 km S of Moustiers. Take D 957. Well-signposted after les Salles.

❖ 83630 Bauduen **Tel** 94 70 05 12 **Rooms** 6 **Prices** FFF
Evening meal by request **Credit Cards** no **Children** yes
Disabled no **Pets** no **Closed** never **Languages** French only
Proprietor Philippe de Santis

Bollène, N of Orange

Château de St-Ariès

If this were a hotel, it would feature in glossy magazines. Set in Italianate gardens, the 150-year-old Tuscan-style villa has a romantic interior: chandeliers, antiques, velvet-covered furniture. Guests dress up for dinner to eat salmon and drink Rhône wines. Up the spiral stone staircase, high-ceilinged bedrooms have pastel walls, antique beds. Fine soaps and 'tons of towels' surround the huge baths. Expensive, elegant and with a genuine welcome that puts many other château owners to shame. Swimming-pool.
Directions 19 km N of Orange. Take N 7, D 26 via Mondragon.

❖ 84500 Bollène **Tel** 90 40 09 17 **Fax** 90 30 45 62 **Rooms** 5 **Prices** FFFF **Evening meal** by request **Credit Cards** MC V **Children** yes **Disabled** no **Pets** yes **Closed** Jan, Feb, mid-Nov to mid-Dec **Languages** English, Italian **Proprietors** Michel de Loÿe

Bonnieux, SW of Apt

La Bouquière

Popular with northern Europeans, the Escobars' attractive renovated home is in a classic country setting. Remote, with stunning views, the house has pale blue shutters, sandy stone walls and terracotta tiles. There is a fireplace in the sitting-room and plenty of books. Bedrooms have private terraces, central heating for the winter, and modern, practical bathrooms. A place to recharge the batteries; restaurant in Bonnieux, 5 minutes away.
Directions 12 km SW of Apt. Take twisting D 3. House is signposted 3 km before Bonnieux.

❖ Quartier St-Pierre, 84480 Bonnieux **Tel** 90 75 87 17 **Rooms** 4 **Prices** FF **Evening meal** no **Credit Cards** no **Children** yes **Disabled** yes **Pets** yes **Closed** never **Languages** English, Spanish **Proprietors** Angel and Françoise Escobar

14 rue de l'Agachon

This carefully restored house in a relatively unspoiled village has been in the family for generations. Bedrooms have white walls, terracotta tiles, exposed beams and country prints. Bathrooms are better than usual, with double wash-basins, plenty of towels, modern furniture. A picture window in the top-floor breakfast *salon* has a magnificent view west towards Fayence across the valley. No nearby car-parking but access is permitted for unloading.
Directions 6 km W of Grasse. Take D 4 to Cabris. Street easy to find.

❖14 rue de l'Agachon, 06530 Cabris **Tel** 93 60 52 36 **Rooms** 5
Prices FF **Evening meal** no **Credit Cards** no **Children** yes
Disabled no **Pets** yes **Closed** Oct, Nov **Languages** French only
Proprietors Jocelyne and Michel Faraut

Courmes, NW of Vence

La Cascade

High on the barren hill behind Vence, overlooking the awesome Gorge du Loup, the Baraccos are young farmers who have created a Spartan spot to stay with 'land, views and space for kids to unwind'. Surprisingly, most visitors are middle-aged couples. Expect no luxuries. Recently redecorated bedrooms, bathrooms and dining-room are neat and tidy. The well-priced evening meal includes their own organically grown vegetables.
Directions 25 km NW of Vence. Take D 2210, D 3 to Bramafan. Steep climb on D 503; 600 m past Courmes on single track road.

❖ 06620 Courmes **Tel** 93 09 65 85 **Rooms** 6 **Prices** FF
Evening meal by request **Credit Cards** V **Children** yes
Disabled no **Pets** yes **Closed** never; telephone in winter
Languages French only **Proprietors** Isabelle and Patrice Baracco

Crillon-le-Brave, NE of Carpentras

Le Clos St-Vincent

This 150-year-old house is set on a hillside with lovely gardens, a large buddleia tree and a swimming-pool. The dovecote even houses real doves. The Venezuelan owner sets guests at ease in his cool, airy but simple home. A Jean Cocteau print hangs in the white-walled sitting-room where dried lavender fills antique scales. One bedroom has white walls, white sheets, a white duvet cover and green-painted furniture. Bathrooms are somewhat basic.
Directions 15 km NE of Carpentras. Take D 974; D 138 left to Crillon. Follow signs.

❖ 84410 Crillon-le-Brave **Tel** 90 65 93 36 **Fax** 90 21 81 46
Rooms 6 **Prices** FFF **Evening meal** Mon, Weds, Fri
Credit Cards no **Children** yes **Disabled** no **Pets** no
Closed mid-Nov to Feb **Languages** English, Spanish
Proprietors Françoise and Vicente Vasquez

Gaja-la-Selve, S of Castelnaudary

La Selve

Raymond Roger deserves to be proud of the renovations he and a friend made to this old house. The ambience is relaxing, with mature oaks, and views of the Pyrenees and endless countryside. The sitting-room and dining-room have cane furniture. Up the curving wooden stairs, the bedrooms have 'typical flowery French wallpaper' plus a bottle of mineral water and chocolates on the pillow. Restaurant 6 km; outdoor swimming-pool.
Directions 16 km S of Castelnaudary. D 6; right on D 47 for St Amans; house on left before Pech-Luna. **Not** in Gaja-la-Selve.

❖ 11270 Gaja-la-Selve **Tel** 68 60 64 69 **Fax** 61 68 12 16 **Rooms** 4
Prices FFF **Evening meal** no **Credit Cards** no **Children** yes
Disabled no **Pets** yes **Closed** mid-Oct to mid-May
Languages French only **Proprietors** Raymond and Andrée Roger

Grimaud, SW of Ste-Maxime

Bastide de l'Avelan

Heavily booked in high summer, this modern house in traditional style is in an open garden. A purple bougainvillaea hangs by the swimming-pool. Part of the long, covered terrace has been glassed-in as a dining area. Bedrooms, separate from the owners' quarters, are whitewashed, brightened with Provençal fabric but quite small. The towels need renewing in the bathrooms. Relaxed and informal but not ideal for children. Above-average prices.

Directions 9 km SW of Ste-Maxime. Take N 98. 1.5 km W of Port Grimaud, on D 14 towards Grimaud. Well-signposted.

❖ Quartier Robert, 83310 Grimaud **Tel** 94 43 25 79 **Rooms** 4 **Prices** FFF **Evening meal** by request **Credit Cards** no **Children** yes **Disabled** no **Pets** no **Closed** never **Languages** English **Proprietors** M and Mme Hermange

Grimaud, SW of St-Maxime

Le Mazet des Mûres

Guests here have the best of both worlds: St Tropez and Port Grimaud are not far away, you can walk to the beach, yet the carefully restored old stone house and outbuildings are in the middle of a field. A huge olive tree stands in front, there are flowers everywhere plus stylish cream sunshades. The ambience is 'away from it all' and there are rave reviews for Mme Decourt's cooking. Guests are international; suitable for families.

Directions 5 km SW of St-Maxime. Take N 98. After 4 km turn right at roundabout to Les Mûres; go up hill, keep right, follow signs.

❖ route du Cros d'Entassi, Quartier Les Mûres, 83360 Grimaud **Tel and Fax** 94 56 44 45 **Rooms** 5 **Prices** FFF **Evening meal** by request **Credit Cards** no **Children** yes **Disabled** no **Pets** no **Closed** never; telephone in winter **Languages** English, German **Proprietors** Brigitte and Jean-Pierre Decourt

Joucas, NW of Apt

Mas de la Soupétrière

In a peaceful valley, this ochre house with its lavender shutters has a swimming-pool, and riding stables for guests who want to explore the surrounding Lubéron National Park. Inside is a mixture of old and new: old beams, tiled floors, modern paintings on plain walls. An English-style breakfast is cooked in the kitchen with its stone fireplace. After an aperitif, the three-course dinner is strictly Provençal, often featuring local lamb.

Directions 14 km NW of Apt. N 100; right on D 4, left on D 2, right on D 102 for Joucas. House is 200 m on right, signposted.

❖ Joucas, 84220 Gordes **Tel** 90 05 78 81 **Fax** 90 05 76 33 **Rooms** 6 **Prices** FFFF **Evening meal** by request **Credit Cards** no **Children** yes **Disabled** no **Pets** yes **Closed** never **Languages** English, German **Proprietor** Christel Hofstadt

L'Isle-sur-la-Sorgue, E of Avignon

La Meridienne

M Tarayre, an artist who works with wood, has made his Provençal home unusually attractive by painting the beams and furniture. The water-colours that brighten the dining-room are by a friend. Ground floor bedrooms open on to private terraces and the garden. All have rough, white walls and simple decoration: blue beams and bedspreads, yellow painted wicker bedheads. A do-as-you-please ambience; fine swimming-pool; kitchen available.

Directions 26 km E of Avignon. Take N 100; 3.5 km beyond L'Isle-sur-la-Sorgue turn left, then left again. Signposted.

❖ Aux Fontanelles, chemin de la Lône, 84800 L'Isle-sur-la-Sorgue **Tel** 90 38 40 26 **Fax** 90 38 58 46 **Rooms** 4 **Prices** FF **Evening meal** no **Credit Cards** no **Children** yes **Disabled** no **Pets** yes **Closed** never **Languages** English, Spanish **Proprietors** Jérôme Tarayre, Muriel Fox

Lacoste, SW of Apt

Bonne Terre

M Lamy has definite ideas about running a bed-and-breakfast. He leaves guests to their own devices: bedrooms are separate from his house; you sign up for breakfast and help yourself; there are even washing facilities. Each of the plain white practical bedrooms has a terrace and fine views. 'Expensive' and 'more like a condominium' are some reactions but it would suit those wanting privacy. Attractive gardens. Swimming-pool.

Directions 16 km SW of Apt. Take N 100 for Avignon. Turn left on D 36, right on D 108. By Renault garage.

❖ Lacoste, 84480 Bonnieux **Tel** 90 75 85 53 **Rooms** 5
Prices FFFF **Evening meal** no **Credit Cards** MC V **Children** yes
Disabled no **Pets** yes **Closed** Nov to Feb **Languages** English,
German **Proprietor** Roland Lamy

Lacoste-en-Lubéron, SW of Apt

Relais du Procureur

This 17thC house verges on being a hotel since palatial bedrooms have television and minibars as well as cream carpets, green and pink curtains, matching bedspreads and old beams. Three have air-conditioning, all have views across to Bonnieux. Down the spiral stone staircase is the sitting-room, with a large fireplace and heavy wooden doors. The swimming-pool fits into a small courtyard. The owner could be more helpful.

Directions 16 km SW of Apt. Take N 100 for Avignon. Turn left on D 36, right on D 108 to Lacoste.

❖ rue Basse, 84710 Lacoste-en-Lubéron **Tel** 90 75 82 28
Fax 90 75 86 94 **Rooms** 7 **Prices** FFFF **Evening meal** no
Credit Cards AE MC V **Children** no **Disabled** no **Pets** no
Closed never **Languages** English, some Italian
Proprietor Antoine Court de Gebelin

Mas du Grand Jonquier

Cherry and mulberry trees surround this former silk farm, opened in 1992. The Grecks, a sophisticated couple, are justifiably proud of their restoration. Bedrooms are modern, with firm mattresses and bright Provençal fabric on bedheads. Old wooden farm implements decorate the stone-walled dining-room. Meals are outstanding: quail with grapes or cherries, steak with Beaumes de Venise wine, chocolate gâteaux, *clafoutis*. Swimming-pool.

Directions 30 km E of Avignon. From N 7 Avignon Sud exit, take D 22. House is 2 km after Petit Palais, near N 100 junction.

❖ 84800 Lagnes **Tel** 90 20 90 13 **Fax** 90 20 91 18 **Rooms** 6
Prices FFF **Evening meal** by request **Credit Cards** MC V
Children yes **Disabled** no **Pets** no **Closed** never
Languages English, German, Italian, Spanish
Proprietors Monique and François Greck

La Pastorale

Antiques are sold in a former carpentry shop; across the courtyard, the converted L-shaped farmhouse has taken guests since 1993. Breakfast is served from 8 am to noon in the suitably rustic dining-room, with white walls and Provençal tablecloths. Bedrooms have bold touches of colour: the blue room has blue bedspreads and wicker chairs, even navy and white towels. This enthusiastic young couple plan a swimming-pool by 1996.

Directions 28 km E of Avignon. Take N 100; bear left on D 99. House is signposted at crossroads with D 24.

❖ route de Fontaine de Vaucluse, Les Gardioles, 84800 Lagnes
Tel 90 20 25 18 **Fax** 90 20 21 86 **Rooms** 4 **Prices** FF
Evening meal no **Credit Cards** no **Children** yes **Disabled** no
Pets yes **Closed** never **Languages** English, German, Italian
Proprietors Elisabeth and Robert Negrel

Les Pins

'You get what you pay for' is true of this 'very ordinary', modern, Provençal-style bungalow with views over the vineyards. Two bedrooms have small terraces, all have stained-pine beds with cushions done up as dolls. Bathrooms are straightforward, clean. The family opened for bed-and-breakfast in 1993 and guests who join them for dinner "eat what we eat". Useful for travellers on a budget or wanting to experience everyday rural life.

Directions 13 km SW of Draguignan. Take D 562 to Lorgues, then D 50 towards St-Antonin. After 4 km, signposted on right.

❖ route de St-Antonin, 83510 Lorgues **Tel** 94 73 91 97 **Rooms** 4
Prices FF **Evening meal** by request **Credit Cards** no
Children yes **Disabled** no **Pets** no **Closed** never
Languages French only **Proprietor** Mme Ghislaine Perin

La Lombarde

The village of Lourmarin is rated one of the prettiest in France, so is often overrun by tourists. La Lombarde is 3 km away, set in lush gardens, though noise from the road can intrude. The swimming-pool is surrounded by natural rock and weeping willows. With self-catering bungalows, this is a professional operation so bedrooms are somewhat plain and bland, but with refrigerators, terraces and modern bathrooms.

Directions 5 km NW of Cadenet. Take D 973 for Lauris. Do not turn right for Lourmarin. House signposted on left.

❖ BP 32, 84160 Lourmarin **Tel** 90 08 40 60 **Fax** 90 08 40 64
Rooms 4 **Prices** FFF **Evening meal** no **Credit Cards** no
Children yes **Disabled** no **Pets** no **Closed** Dec to Easter
Languages English, Spanish **Proprietors** Eva and Gilbert Lèbre

Lourmarin, N of Cadenet

Villa St-Louis

Renovated in 1990, this former police station and post house has a terrace above the street, shaded by a tree and white curtains that billow in a breeze. Interior decorator Michel filled the rooms with antiques and collectables: a 19thC bed, old paintings, a birdcage. Too cluttered for some tastes, it is not suitable for small children. Guests help themselves to breakfast in the sitting-room/kitchen/dining-room. We would like to see some new towels.
Directions 5 km N of Cadenet. Take D 943 to Lourmarin. Easy to find.

❖ 35 rue H de Savournin, 84160 Lourmarin **Tel** 90 68 39 18
Fax 90 68 10 07 **Rooms** 5 **Prices** FF **Evening meal** no
Credit Cards no **Children** yes **Disabled** no **Pets** yes
Closed never **Languages** English **Proprietors** Bernadette and
Michel Lasalette

Malemort-du-Comtat, SE of Carpentras

Château d'Unang

This is a château where guests may feel more tolerated than welcome. The building is elegant but the driveway needs weeding, stone steps need replacing. A stuffed penguin and the smell of polish are reminders of yesteryear. Bedrooms have marble fireplaces, vast mirrors. Bathrooms are spacious but towels are thin. Breakfast and (expensive) dinners are served at separate tables; the hostess never eats with guests. Swimming-pool.
Directions 14 km SE of Carpentras. Take D 4 for Venasque; left on D 5. House on right 3 km beyond Malemort towards Méthamis.

❖ 84570 Malemort-du-Comtat **Tel** 90 69 71 06 **Fax** 90 69 92 80
Rooms 4 **Prices** FFFF **Evening meal** by request **Credit Cards** MC
V **Children** no **Disabled** no **Pets** no **Closed** Jan, Feb
Languages English, Spanish **Proprietor** Marie Lefer

Menton

Victoria

In this sophisticated resort, with its long tradition of British visitors, the lively owner's home is right in the middle of town, but set back in gardens, away from the traffic. One bedroom has its own television, refrigerator and sitting area since many visitors book in for a week at a time. Longer stays receive a discount. The other rooms share a sitting-room with television. Breakfast is in the garden. The private parking is a major bonus.

Directions in the middle of Menton, a few steps from Tourist Office.

❖ 14 avenue Boyer, 06500 Menton **Tel** 93 28 42 49 **Rooms** 3
Prices FF **Evening meal** no **Credit Cards** no **Children** no
Disabled no **Pets** no **Closed** never **Languages** English, Italian,
Spanish, some German **Proprietor** Anna Bret

Mollégès, E of St-Rémy-de-Provence

Mas de l'Ange

One partner is a designer, the other makes furniture, so the Lafforgues' conversion has transformed an ordinary 60-year-old farmhouse into a stylish rural retreat, complete with orchards and corral. Bedrooms have plenty of homey touches such as a photo album, a pair of red, rope-soled sandals, some seashells and even a boat to play with in the bath. Pottery bowls of lemons and rose petals make it look very Provençale.

Directions 11 km E of St-Rémy-de-Provence on D 31. Look for signs 3 km before Mollégès.

❖ Petite Route de St-Rémy-de-Provence, 13940 Mollégès
Tel 90 95 08 33 **Fax** 90 95 48 69 **Rooms** 5 **Prices** FFF-FFFF
Evening meal no **Credit Cards** no **Children** yes **Disabled** no
Pets yes **Closed** never **Languages** French only
Proprietors Hélène and Bruno Lafforgue

Montmaur, SE of Toulouse

La Castagne

This is popular with families who like the swings, play area, pony rides and sheltered swimming-pool. A bedroom has been opened recently in an old barn; the original beams survive. The second guest bedroom is upstairs in the main house, with an extra double bed for children in a curtained-off alcove. Jacqueline Martin's cooking is ample and delicious, as Michel's girth testifies.

Directions 50 km SE of Toulouse. A 61 for Carcassonne. Exit at Villefranche-du-Lauragais. N 113, SE for Avignonet. Left on D 43. Right after 7 km to Montmaur. Follow signs in village.

❖ 11320 Montmaur **Tel** 68 60 00 40 **Rooms** 2 **Prices** FF
Evening meal by request **Credit Cards** no **Children** yes
Disabled no **Pets** yes **Closed** Dec to March **Languages** English,
Spanish **Proprietors** Jacqueline and Michel Martin

Mormoiron, E of Carpentras

Portail Vieux

The owners are British, so the square, pink house is a mix of cultures: a bicycle and birdcage sprout flowers, a sewing-table displays dried wildflowers. The young couple, who have two children, organise painting courses. Furniture is ancient and modern, French and English. Some is painted Provençal-style. The atmosphere is informal, though dinner is a candle-lit affair which is well-priced with regional dishes. Not French, but fun.

Directions 12 km E of Carpentras. Take D 942 from Carpentras towards Sault. Village is on left. House is by bridge, signposted.

❖ 84570 Mormoiron **Tel** 90 61 80 34 **Fax** 90 61 97 55 **Rooms** 7
Prices FF **Evening meal** by request **Credit Cards** no
Children yes **Disabled** yes **Pets** yes **Closed** never
Languages English, German, French **Proprietors** Chantal and
Robin Ochs

Paradou, SW of Les Baux

La Burlande

Well-known as a quality bed-and-breakfast, the large secluded house has delightful grounds. A gardener tends the sloping lawn, rose-covered pergola, flower beds and rockery by the large swimming-pool. Children may use the swings and slide "as long as they are well-behaved." The hosts are sophisticated. Bedrooms are elegant but plain, almost hotel-like with televisions and terraces. The laundry service is useful. Lunch in summer.

Directions 4 km SW of Les Baux-de-Provence. Take D 78 F for Fontvieille, then third left on CM 83, a rural track.

❖ 13520 Paradou **Tel** 90 54 32 32 **Rooms** 4 **Prices** FF
Evening meal by request **Credit Cards** no **Children** yes
Disabled no **Pets** yes **Closed** never **Languages** English, German
Proprietors Pierre and Jenny Fajardo de Livry

Pont-de-Barret, E of Montélimar

Les Tuillères

John Williams is a professional photographer who teaches enthusiasts how and where to point their cameras. He and his wife converted a 300-year-old *bastide* (fortified farmhouse) and offer bed-and-breakfast. The stone buildings are roomy, with wood beams, galleries and mantelpieces. The bedrooms, on two floors, are well-furnished, with central heating. Meals are authentically French. Swimming-pool, stream in rambling grounds.

Directions 30 km E of Montélimar. Take D 940, D 540 to la Bégude. Left on D 9; right at Charols on D 128 to village. Signposted.

❖ 26160 Pont-de-Barret **Tel** 75 90 43 91 **Rooms** 5 **Prices** FF
Evening meal yes **Credit Cards** no **Children** yes **Disabled** no
Pets no **Closed** never **Languages** English **Proprietors** John and
Yvonne Williams

Pontevès, NE of St-Maximin

Domaine de St-Ferréol

The owner is a wine grower and local historian. His family have lived here for 150 years but the house is a century older, with a massive sandstone doorway in the best guest-room. Others are somewhat cramped. All are in one wing and have white walls, waxed wood, exposed beams, traditional textiles. Breakfast and Provençal-style dinners are served in the hosts' dining-room, though guests may prepare simple meals in a small kitchen.

Directions 24 km NE of St-Maximin. Take D 560. House is on left, 3 km beyond Barjols, still on D 560.

❖ 83670 Pontevès **Tel** 94 77 10 42 **Fax** 94 77 19 04
Rooms 4 **Prices** FF **Evening meal** by request **Credit Cards** no
Children yes **Disabled** no **Pets** no **Closed** never
Languages English, German, some Spanish
Proprietors Armelle and Guillaume de Jerphanion

Puicheric, E of Carcassonne

Château de St-Aunay

Not every French wine château is old: when the owners needed to renovate their 1907 home in the Minervois vineyards, bed-and-breakfast guests helped to pay the bills. Five years on, there are six light, airy bedrooms which are full in summer when guests stay for a week at a time. Jean-Pierre is proud of his wines and his wife's cooking: *poulet aux langoustines* and *cassoulet*. Swimming-pool, swings in the garden.

Directions 25 km E of Carcassonne. Take N 113, D 610. Just before Puicheric, turn left on D 111. House on right, past bridge.

❖ 1700 Puicheric **Tel** 68 43 72 20 **Rooms** 6 **Prices** FF
Evening meal by request **Credit Cards** no **Children** yes
Disabled no **Pets** yes **Closed** mid-Oct to mid-April
Languages some English, Spanish **Proprietors** Simone and Jean-Pierre Berge

Ramatuelle

Leï Souco

A veteran in French bed-and-breakfast terms, Mme Giraud has taken guests for some 25 years. Set in vineyards, olive and eucalyptus trees, her modern Provençale-style house on the St-Tropez peninsula is a haven from the crowded coast. Bedrooms and bathrooms are exceptionally large with their own entrances and terraces. Whitewashed walls, rustic but comfortable furniture plus refrigerators and safes. A tennis-court. Restaurants nearby.

Directions 2 km from Ramatuelle. Take D 93 towards St-Tropez. House is 200 m up drive, next to Total station on right.

❖ Plaine de Camarat, 83350 Ramatuelle **Tel** 94 79 80 22
Rooms 8 **Prices** FFF **Evening meal** no **Credit Cards** no
Children yes **Disabled** no **Pets** yes **Closed** Oct to Easter
Languages some English **Proprietors** M and Mme Gustave Giraud

St-Martin-les-Eaux, NW of Manosque

Domaine d'Aurouze

Deep in the Luberon and hard to find. The Masselots make dinner part of the price; lunch, however, is an optional extra. Few guests want to leave this modernised, ochre-stone *bastide* (fortified house) which dates from 1623 and is full of antiques and paintings. Cécile has a reputation for her cookery, which uses organic ingredients. Bedrooms and bathrooms are equally luxurious; in high season the minimum is a week's stay.

Directions 20 km NW of Manosque via N 96, D 13. Turn off at Dauphin. Between Notre-Dame d'Ubage Chapel and St-Martin.

❖ 04870 St-Martin-les-Eaux **Tel** 92 87 66 51 **Fax** 92 87 56 35
Rooms 3 **Prices** FFFF **Evening meal** obligatory **Credit Cards** no
Children yes **Disabled** yes **Pets** no **Closed** Nov to late March
Languages English, German, Italian, Spanish, Arabic
Proprietors Didier and Cécile Masselot

Vaison-la-Romaine, NE of Orange

L'Evêché

Local guide books in the little sitting-room and tips on nearby restaurants are just part of the Verdiers' welcome. In the old part of town, the 500-year-old, former bishop's palace has been reno-vated over the past 15 years by this couple who serve breakfast on a terrace overlooking the mountains. Expect home-made blueberry jam and coffee in white china pots. Bright Provençal prints liven up the small whitewashed bedrooms.

Directions 35 km NE of Orange on D 977. Rue de l'Evêché is in the heart of the old, medieval district.

❖ Rue de l'Evêché, Ville Médiévale, 84110 Vaison-la-Romaine **Tel** 90 36 13 46 **Fax** 90 36 32 43 **Rooms** 4 **Prices** FFF **Evening meal** no **Credit Cards** no **Children** yes **Disabled** no **Pets** yes **Closed** never **Languages** English **Proprietors** Aude and Jean-Loup Verdier

Vaison-la-Romaine, NE of Orange

Quartier le Brusquet

The Delesses are retired and host just one set of house guests at a time. Their pale stone home is large, with lavender along the dri-veway. The white walled hallway is hung with pictures. The bed-room, with separate entrance, has sliding glass doors to a terrace with mountain views. The bathroom is jazzy: pink and purple tiles, blue taps. Breakfast is in the courtyard or in the somewhat clut-tered dining-room. Swimming-pool.

Directions 35 km NE of Orange. Take N 7, D 977. In Vaison-la-Romaine, behind the football stadium.

❖ chemin de l'Ioou, 84110 Vaison-la-Romaine **Tel** 90 36 38 38 **Rooms** 1 **Prices** FF **Evening meal** no **Credit Cards** no **Children** yes **Disabled** yes **Pets** yes **Closed** 3 weeks in July **Languages** English, German **Proprietors** Claude and François Delesse

Maison aux Volets Bleus

Formerly chef-owners of a small hotel, the Marets have recreated the popular image of Provence: dried flowers hang from the ceiling of the communal sitting-room, a fountain tinkles in the shaded courtyard where simple dishes like *daube provençale* are served, with local cheeses and wines. In one of France's prettiest villages, this 17thC house has some bedrooms with views of Mont Ventoux. A *trompe l'oeil* screen hides the courtyard.

Directions 10 km SE of Carpentras on D 4. Place des Bouviers is off the Place de la Fontaine.

❖ Place des Bouviers, Le Village, 84210 Venasque
Tel 90 66 03 04 **Fax** 90 66 16 14 **Rooms** 6 **Prices** FFF
Evening meal by request **Credit Cards** no **Children** yes
Disabled no **Pets** yes **Closed** mid-Nov to Feb **Languages** English
Proprietors Martine and Jérôme Maret

Quartier du Camp Long

The Borel family are veterans of the bed-and-breakfast business, having been open for nearly 20 years. Their main livelihood is growing cherries, so they close in June. The rest of the year guests return 'like friends' to the simple, rather old-fashioned rooms, happy to lounge around the swimming-pool in the July and August heat. Roses grow up the side of the farmhouse, set high in the rocky hills with impressive views. A relaxing, unpretentious spot.

Directions 10 km SE of Carpentras. Take D 4 to Venasque. Well-signposted but useful to ask for directions.

❖ Quartier du Camp Long, 84210 Venasque **Tel and Fax** 90 66 03 56 **Rooms** 5 **Prices** FF **Evening meal** no **Credit Cards** no **Children** yes **Disabled** yes **Pets** no **Closed** June
Languages French only **Proprietors** Marie-France and Régis Borel

Vernoux-en-Vivarais, W of Valence

Ferme de Prémaure

On a hillside in the rural, northern Ardèche, this 1820 stone farmhouse has been carefully converted by the Achards who also breed horses. The former stable wing has small, comfortable bedrooms: some are split-level, all have modern but rustic furniture with exposed beams. Bathrooms are small but adequate. One guest comes to write; others bring children. Claudine is a fine cook; dinners are eaten communally at long tables.

Directions 36 km W of Valence. Take twisting D 533, D 14 to Vernoux, D 2 to Lamastre. Farm signposted on right after 8 km.

❖ route de Lamastre, 07240 Vernoux-en-Vivarais
Tel 75 58 16 61 **Rooms** 9 **Prices** FFF **Evening meal** by request
Credit Cards no **Children** yes **Disabled** no **Pets** no
Closed mid-Nov to Easter **Languages** some English
Proprietors Roland and Claudine Achard

Villeneuve-de-Berg, SE of Aubenas

Le Mas de Fournery

Run more like a small hotel, this 400-year-old farmhouse encloses a flowery courtyard. Bedrooms, all with television, mini-bars and telephones, are plain, rustic but comfortable with tiled floors and bright, modern bathrooms. One has wheelchair access. The restaurant, with elaborate dishes, serves lunch and dinner to the public. High enough for views of five *départements*, there is a swimming-pool and a *vinothèque* (wine cellar) for socializing.

Directions 16 km SE of Aubenas. Take N 102 to Villeneuve; D 259 for St-Andéol. Take first right after chapel, up drive.

❖ route de St-Andéol-de-Berg, 07170 Villeneuve-de-Berg
Tel 75 94 83 73 **Rooms** 5 **Prices** FFF **Evening meal** by request
Credit Cards MC V **Children** yes **Disabled** yes **Pets** yes
Closed Dec to Feb **Languages** English, German
Proprietors Philippe Klaiss and family

➠ *More on page 194*

Calvello-Patrimonio, W of Bastia

Château Calvello

A cannon ball in the wall recalls the French siege of this former fortress whose cheerful owner insists on guests taking half-board. Well-priced, this includes dinners of traditional Corsican dishes: her son's *charcuterie* and *bouillabaisse*, lamb with aubergines and lemons, then *fiadone*, a *fromage frais* and lemon dessert. Breakfast brings orange juice in crystal glasses, embroidered napkins, crêpes. Bedrooms have television and a refrigerator.

Directions 18 km W of Bastia. Take mountainous D 81 to Patrimonio. Follow signs.

❖ 20253 Patrimonio **Tel** 95 37 01 15 **Rooms** 2 **Prices** FFF **Evening meal** obligatory **Credit Cards** no **Children** no **Disabled** no **Pets** no **Closed** never **Languages** Italian **Proprietors** M and Mme Pierre-Louis Ficaja

San Gavino, NW of Bonifacio

Chez Bartoli

Since 1992, Mme Bartoli has offered two plain, practical rooms in the nearby modern house of her sister, an English teacher. Meals, however, are in her own granite ancestral home. Corsican favourites prepared "like my grandmother's," include vegetable and ham-bone soup, game in autumn. She uses *brocciu*, a local *fromage frais*, in omelettes, cakes, pancakes and *cannelloni*. The remote hamlet is a base for walkers. Unspoilt beaches are 6 km away.

Directions 20 km NW of Bonifacio. Take N 196; turn right for Poggiale on D 22. Signposted on left.

❖ 20170 San Gavino **Tel** 95 71 01 29 **Rooms** 2 **Prices** FF **Evening meal** by request **Credit Cards** no **Children** yes **Disabled** no **Pets** no **Closed** never **Languages** French only **Proprietors** Bartoli family

➡ *More on page 198*

Bayeux

Château Le Castel

Set in a spacious park, Baron d'Avray's 18thC château is surprisingly quiet despite being within walking distance of Bayeux's Tapestry and museums. Bedrooms are comfortable and elegant. One suite is particularly well-priced for a week's stay.

Directions rue de la Gambette is off rue St-Loup in SW part of old town.

❖ 7 rue de la Gambette, 14400 Bayeux **Tel** 31 92 05 86 **Fax** 31 92 55 64 **Rooms** 4 **Prices** FFF **Evening meal** no **Credit Cards** no **Children** yes **Closed** never; telephone in winter **Languages** English

Beuvron-en-Auge, E of Caen

Chalet Normand

This old village, a photogenic mixture of brick and half-timbering, is crowded on fine weekends but guests at Jacqueline Fouquet's house enjoy the ambience once the tourists have gone. Simple, family-style bedrooms. Three restaurants within walking distance.

Directions 30 km E of Caen. Take N 175, D 49. House is on main street of Beuvron-en-Auge.

❖ Beuvron-en-Auge, 14430 Dozulé **Tel** 31 39 02 57 **Rooms** 3 **Prices** FF **Evening meal** no **Credit Cards** no **Children** yes **Closed** never **Languages** some English

Bures-sur-Dives, E of Caen

Manoir des Tourpes

Close to the ferries and the Auge valley, the 300-year-old grey stone manor house, with elegant antiques and 11thC ghost, is in parkland on the Dives river. American Michael Cassady and Marie-Cathérine Landon serve an English tea. No pets.

Directions 14 km E of Caen. Take N 175 to Troarn. Left on D 95 to Bures-sur-Dives. House signposted, by river.

❖ rue de l'Eglise, 14670 Bures-sur-Dives **Tel** 31 23 63 47 **Fax** 31 23 86 10 **Rooms** 2 **Prices** FF **Evening meal** no **Credit Cards** no **Children** yes **Closed** never **Languages** English

Carnac

Le Ranguhan

Mme Le Moing says that bed-and-breakfast is "their life" nowadays. The white-painted house is neat and the garden well-tended, but the interior is rather dull. The hosts live nearby at Lorient. An economical base for Carnac's stones.

Directions Some 500 m from Carnac Tourist Information Office. Signposted.

❖ 56340 Carnac **Tel** 97 52 04 82 or 97 83 06 21 **Rooms** 3 **Prices** FF **Evening meal** no **Credit Cards** no **Children** no **Closed** Oct to Easter **Languages** French only

---

Carquefou, NE of Nantes
Château Le Housseau

The Audonnet's 15thC manor house on the outskirts of Nantes is smothered in creeper. Upgraded and transformed into a luxurious place to stay, it is also expensive. Breakfast is extra but aperitifs and wines are included in the price of a candle-lit meal.
Directions 6 km NE of Nantes. Take D 178 to Carquefou. Follow signs to château.

❖ 44470 Carquefou **Tel** 40 30 21 95 **Rooms** 5 **Prices** FFFF **Evening meal** by request **Credit Cards** V **Children** yes **Closed** never **Languages** English

---

Champfleur, SE of Alençon
La Garancière

This 100-year-old farmhouse has nothing special in the way of bedrooms, but the Langlais family enjoy taking in guests. One room has an outside staircase; another, in a separate building, has a ground floor room, recently redecorated.
Directions 5 km SE of Alençon. Take N 138 S towards Le Mans. Take D 55 left to Champfleur.

❖ 72610 Champfleur **Tel** 33 31 75 84 **Rooms** 5 **Prices** FF **Evening meal** by request **Credit Cards** V **Children** yes **Closed** never **Languages** English

---

Chartres
25 rue du Bourg

For over a decade, Yves Bothorel has offered what are really self-contained flats: plain rooms, small bathrooms, self-service breakfast. Handy for the sights. Views of river. Useful for budget-conscious visitors.
Directions a few steps downhill, E of the Cathedral and towards the Eure River.

❖ 25 rue du Bourg, 28000 Chartres **Tel** 37 34 66 38 **Rooms** 2 **Prices** FF **Evening meal** no **Credit Cards** no **Children** yes **Closed** mid-Sept to mid-May **Languages** French only

---

Cottun, SW of Bayeux
Château de Cottun

Handy for Bayeux and the D-Day Beaches, the Lenormand family's impressive country mansion has six luxurious bedrooms, with television, in the main house. Rooms in the annexe are less expensive but comfortable. Business-like. Swimming-pool, large park.
Directions 5 km SW of Bayeux. Take D 5. Cottun signposted on right. Clearly marked.

❖ 14400 Cottun **Tel** 31 92 41 55 **Fax** 31 22 43 02 **Rooms** 12 **Prices** FF **Evening meal** by request **Credit Cards** V **Children** yes **Closed** mid-Sept to Easter **Languages** English

---

Douarnenez-Pouldavid

Kerleguer

The Larours are a welcoming retired couple with a country small-holding near Douarnenez, which is more port than resort. Clean bedrooms, efficient showers, some mosquitoes in summer. Swim at Pointe du Raz, eat in Locronan. Useful on a tight budget.

Directions 1 km SW of Douarnenez. Take D 765; as soon as you leave built-up area, look for signs on right to farm.

❖ 29100 Douarnenez **Tel** 98 92 34 64 **Rooms** 3 **Prices** FF
Evening meal no **Credit Cards** no **Children** yes **Closed** never
Languages French only

Géfosse-Fontenay, NW of Bayeux

L'Hermerel

Agnès and François Lemarie converted the 15thC chapel of their stone farmhouse into a sitting-room. The bedrooms are plain but two can sleep five people. Set in fields near the sea, restaurants are within 3 km. Well-priced, with atmospheric dining-room.

Directions 32 km NW of Bayeux. Take N 13 to Osmanville; turn right on D 514, left on D 199a. Look for 'L'Hermerel' sign.

❖ 14230 Géfosse-Fontenay **Tel** 31 22 64 12 **Rooms** 4 **Prices** FF
Evening meal no **Credit Cards** no **Children** yes **Closed** never
Languages English, German

Géfosse-Fontenay, NW of Bayeux

La Rivière

In a fortified stone farmhouse by the sea, Isabelle Leharivel's evening meals of Norman specialities are bargain-priced. The dining-room has beams and a huge fireplace. One bedroom is on the ground floor. Use of a small kitchen. No pets.

Directions 32 km NW of Bayeux. Take N 13 to Osmanville; turn right on D 514, left on D 199a to village. Signposted on left.

❖ 14230 Géfosse-Fontenay **Tel** 31 22 64 45 **Rooms** 5 **Prices** FF
Evening meal by request **Credit Cards** no **Children** yes
Closed never **Languages** English

Kerdruc, S of Pont-Aven

Pen Ker Dagorn

Don't be put off by the profusion of signs around the white-painted entrance gate. The owner of the stone country villa has excellent taste and the three bedrooms are spacious and well-furnished. Book well in advance in high summer.

Directions 5 km S of Pont-Aven. Take D 77 to Nevez. Follow clear signs to Kerdruc.

❖ Chemin des Vieux-Fours, 29920 Kerdruc **Tel** 98 06 85 01
Rooms 3 **Prices** FF **Evening meal** no **Credit Card** no **Children** yes
Closed Nov to March **Languages** French only

Maisons, NW of Bayeux

Manoir du Carel

Between Bayeux and the coast, this stone country house was once a fortress. The Aumond family have redecorated without spoiling the historic atmosphere but the plumbing is contemporary. A separate cottage in the grounds is useful for families.
Directions 5.5 km NW of Bayeux. Take D 6; turn left to Maisons. House on right after 1 km.

❖ Maisons, 14400 Bayeux **Tel** 31 22 37 00 **Fax** 31 21 57 00
Rooms 4 **Prices** FFF **Evening meal** no **Credit Cards** MC V
Children yes **Closed** never **Languages** English

Manvieux, N of Bayeux

Les Jardins

Gilberte Martragny's small, 18thC stone farmhouse has been in her family for generations. Tastefully renovated, the large bedrooms have old beams but modern comforts, separate entrances. Breakfast in the library. Tennis-court on site. Restaurants 2 km.
Directions 10 km N of Bayeux. Take D 516; left on D 514. Signposted 'Les Jardins' beyond Manvieux.

❖ 4117 Manvieux **Tel** 31 21 95 17 **Rooms** 2 **Prices** FFF
Evening meal no **Credit Cards** no **Children** yes **Closed** never
Languages French only

Monts-en-Bessin, SW of Caen

La Varinière La Vallée

The Edneys are British but their well-priced evening meals offer authentic Normandy dishes. They redecorated, using pretty matching curtains and wallpaper, quality antique furniture. The sitting-room has a television and large open fire. Value for money.
Directions 22 km SW of Caen. N 175, then sharp right on D 6 before Villers-Bocage. Right on D 92 to Monts-en-Bessin. Signposted.

❖ 14310 Monts-en-Bessin **Tel** 31 77 44 73 **Rooms** 5 **Prices** FF
Evening meal by request **Credit Cards** no **Children** yes
Closed never **Languages** English

Pertheville-Ners, E of Falaise

Le Chêne Sec

The main house on this working farm dates from the 15thC. Inside are stone floors, beams, antiques and a large fireplace. The spacious but plain bedrooms have new beds, mattresses. Mme Plassais insists that breakfast is taken by 9 am. Well-priced.
Directions 10 km E of Falaise. Take D 63. Turn right to Ners, then Pertheville-Ners. Signposted.

❖14700 Pertheville-Ners **Tel** 31 90 17 55 **Rooms** 3 **Prices** FF
Evening meal no **Credit Cards** no **Children** yes **Closed** never
Languages some English

Pleugueneuc, SE of Dinan

Château de la Bourbansais

20 km south-east of Dinan, the young Comte de Lorgeril runs one of Brittany's finest châteaux. A night in one of the luxurious suites does not come cheaply. There is also a zoo and collection of classic American cars in the grounds.

Directions Pleugueneuc is on the N 137 Rennes to St Malo road. Follow signs to the château from the village.

❖ 35720 Pleugueneuc **Tel** 99 69 40 07 **Rooms** 2 **Prices** FFFF **Evening meal** by request **Credit Cards** AE DC MC V **Children** no **Closed** Nov to Easter **Languages** English, German

---

Pommerit-Jaudy, NW of Guingamp

Quillevez Vraz

Georges Beauverger's home, surrounded by neat gardens, is inland, but guests are happy to drive just a few minutes' to the sea. Bedrooms are in a separate building, with cooking facilities for picnics, evening meals. Heavily booked in summer.

Directions 20 km NW of Guingamp. Take D 8. Look for signs in village.

❖ 22450 Pommerit-Jaudy **Tel** 96 91 35 74 **Rooms** 3 **Prices** FF **Evening meal** no **Credit Cards** no **Children** yes **Closed** never **Languages** English

---

Quiberville, W of Dieppe

Le Village

The Auclerts' late-19thC brick country home is quiet, at the end of an avenue of chestnut trees in a traditional Norman seaside resort. Bedrooms are large, with antiques. Games are available for children. Somewhat expensive. Nearest restaurants 1 km away.

Directions 18 km W of Dieppe. Take D 925. Exact directions given when booking.

❖ rue des Vergers, 76860 Quiberville **Tel** 35 83 16 10 **Rooms** 5 **Prices** FFF **Evening meal** no **Credit Cards** no **Children** no **Closed** never **Languages** English

---

Riec-sur-Belon, SE of Pont-Aven

Kéraval

Mme Guillemot, a kindly grandmother, has a clean Breton farmhouse with a dog, cat and rabbits. Some country dampness in bedrooms but breakfast, says a visitor, can be a 'fun French and Breton language lesson'. Useful for families on a budget.

Directions 5 km SE of Pont-Aven. Take D 783 to Riec; turn left on D 104. Turn right after 1 km, up farm lane. Signposted.

❖ 29340 Riec-sur-Belon **Tel** 98 06 94 43 **Rooms** 2 **Prices** FF **Evening meal** no **Credit Cards** no **Children** yes **Closed** never **Languages** French only

---

La Bergerie

Jacky and Jocelyne Piel recently took advantage of their proximity to Mont-St-Michel to open this hotel-like bed-and-breakfast. All bedrooms look the same. The breakfast-room has a cold atmosphere with separate tables, like a café.
Directions 8 km NW of Pontorson. Take D 797 through Roz-sur-Couesnon to La Poultière. Follow signs.

❖ La Poultière, 35610 Roz-sur-Couesnon **Tel** 99 80 29 68 **Rooms** 5 **Prices** FF **Evening meal** no **Credit Cards** no **Children** yes **Closed** never **Languages** French only

---

La Roselierre

Near Mont-St-Michel. The profusion of flowers is misleading. In a separate building, bedrooms have bare walls, linoleum floors, shiny blue bedspreads. Bathrooms, like swimming-pool changing-rooms, have bench seats. One has disabled facilities.
Directions 6 km NW of Pontorson. Take D 797. House on main road of village.

❖ 35610 Roz-sur-Couesnon **Tel** 99 80 22 05 **Rooms** 5 **Prices** FF **Evening meal** by request **Credit Cards** no **Children** yes **Closed** mid-Nov to Easter **Languages** French only

---

La Gautrais

We were disappointed by the lack of comfort at this modernised farmhouse: old-fashioned wallpaper, sparse bedrooms, odd towels. Catherine Tiffaine cooks well and has taken guests for over a decade but the location is right by the road.
Directions 20 km S of Avranches. Take N 276, D 998 to St-James. On D 12, 1.5 km towards Antrain.

❖ 50240 St-James **Tel** 33 48 31 86 **Rooms** 4 **Prices** FF **Evening meal** by request **Credit Cards** no **Children** yes **Closed** never **Languages** some English

---

La Bussière

Ivy climbs this country house with its high-pitched, tiled roof and tall mansard windows. Antoine Le Brethon is a lively hostess who offers two well-priced evening menus. Prettily decorated bedrooms have antiques. Some guests bring their own horses.
Directions 17 km W of l'Aigle. Take N 26. Signposted on left, 1 km after Ste-Gauburge-Ste-Colombe.

❖ 61370 Ste-Gauburge-Ste-Colombe **Tel** 33 34 05 23 **Rooms** 2 **Prices** FF **Evening meal** by request **Credit Cards** no **Children** yes **Closed** never **Languages** English, German

---

Le Sap, N of Gacé

Les Roches

A working farm in Normandy, with the half-timbering typical of the area. Gérard Bourgault and his wife enjoy hosting families looking for well-priced accommodation: all three bedrooms now have private baths; spare beds available. Hearty evening meals.
Directions 15 km N of Gacé. Take N 138; turn left at Monnai crossroad. Well signposted before Le Sap on D 12.

❖ 61470 Le Sap **Tel** 33 39 47 39 **Rooms** 3 **Prices** FF
Evening meal by request **Credit Cards** no **Children** yes
Closed never **Languages** French only.

La Turballe, NW of La Baule

Ker Kayenne

Colette Pommereuil's sturdy, square stone home is usually full in the height of the summer season thanks to her comfortable bedrooms, the large heated swimming-pool in the tidy garden and her own warm welcome.
Directions 12 km NW of La Baule. Take D 99 to village. House 500 m on right after the Quatre Routes crossroads.

❖ boulevard de Lauvergnac, 44420 La Turballe **Tel** 40 62 84 30
Fax 40 62 83 38 **Rooms** 6 **Prices** FF **Evening meal** by request
Credit Cards no **Children** yes **Closed** never **Languages** French only

---

Vergoncey, S of Avranches

Ferme de l'Etang Bouceel

Most visitors choose to stay here because the Gavards' home is so close to Mont-St-Michel. They return because of Brigitte's cooking and the views over the lake. The bedrooms upstairs are quite large, with a third bed, and are particularly well-priced.
Directions 15 km S of Avranches. Take N 276, D 40, left to Bouceel on D 308. Not in Vergoncey.

❖ Bouceel, 50240 Vergoncey **Tel** 33 48 34 68 **Rooms** 4 **Prices** FF
Evening meal by request **Credit Cards** no **Children** yes
Closed never **Languages** French only

Vouilly, W of Bayeux

Le Château

The Hamels' white stone mansion is more relaxed than many château-style bed-and-breakfasts, so it is busy in summer. Families enjoy the large garden but dinner is 4 km away in a *ferme auberge* or 8 km in a restaurant. Well-priced.
Directions 30 km W of Bayeux. Take N 13 to la Cambe. Left on D 113 via Montreville. House on left on entry to Vouilly.

❖ 14230 Vouilly **Tel** 31 22 08 59 **Fax** 31 22 90 58 **Rooms** 5
Prices FF **Evening meal** no **Credit Cards** no **Children** yes
Closed Dec to Feb **Languages** English

Le Châtelet-en-Brie, E of Melun

16 Grande Rue

The attractive small farmhouse with a garden and comfortable bedrooms is in the hamlet of La Borde near the A 5. Nadine and Yves Guérif provide a useful base for Euro Disney and Fontainebleau. Regular trains to Paris from Melun. Pets welcome.
Directions 12 km E of Melun. Take D 408, then bear right on D 47 E to La Borde. Next to Mairie (town hall).

❖ 16 Grande Rue, La Borde, 77820 Le Châtelet-en-Brie
Tel 1 60 66 60 54 **Rooms** 3 **Prices** FF **Evening meal** by request
Credit Cards no **Children** yes **Closed** never **Languages** English

---

Dammarie-les-Lys, SW of Melun

La Ferme de Vosves

Georges Lemarchand is a farmer; his wife, Geneviève, is an artist who teaches water-colour painting. Her works enliven their pretty farmhouse with its red tiles and creeper. One bedroom, the 'studio', has old beams; the other is a suite. Restaurants nearby.
Directions 7 km SW of Melun. Take N 372; turn right on N 472 to hamlet of Vosves.

❖ 155 rue de Boississe, Vosves, 77190 Dammarie-les-Lys
Tel 1 64 39 22 28 **Rooms** 2 **Prices** FF **Evening meal** no
Credit Cards no **Children** yes **Closed** never **Languages** English, Italian

---

Herbeville, W of Paris

2 rue de Maule

Useful as a base for exploring Paris and local attractions such as Versailles. Mme Louise Turmel is used to having overseas visitors in her pseudo-Louis XV suburban villa with its swimming-pool, tennis-court. Always telephone ahead of time.
Directions 34 km W of Paris. Take A 13, exit at Poissy. Take D 45 to Herbeville. House at entrance to Herbeville.

❖ 2 rue de Maule, 78580 Herbeville **Tel** 1 30 90 65 22 **Rooms** 4
Prices FFF **Evening meal** no **Credit Cards** no **Children** yes
Closed never **Languages** French only

Moigny-sur-Ecole, W of Fontainebleau

10 sentier de la Grille

Mme Appel's recently renovated stone house has a suite (two bedrooms with connecting bathroom) on the ground floor. This looks out onto her garden which guests may use. A relaxing base for visiting Fontainebleau or Paris (48 km). Restaurant 3 km.
Directions 23 km W of Fontainebleau. Take D 409 to Milly-la-Forêt. Right on D 948. In Moigny-sur-Ecole.

❖ 10 sentier de la Grille, 91490 Moigny-sur-Ecole **Tel** 1 64 98 49 97
Rooms 2 **Prices** FF **Evening meal** no **Credit Cards** no
Children yes **Closed** never **Languages** English, Spanish

Neufmoutiers-en-Brie, E of Paris

Bellevue

An elegant 19thC country mansion just a 10-minute drive from Euro Disney. Isabelle and Patrick Galpin have split-level bedrooms, all clean and modern. Guests praise the breakfasts for quantity and variety, evening meals for value for money.
Directions 40 km E of Paris. Take N 4. After Tournan-en-Brie, left on D 96 to Neufmoutiers-en-Brie. Signposted in village.

❖ 77610 Neufmoutiers-en-Brie **Tel** 1 64 07 11 05 **Fax** 1 64 07 19 27
Rooms 5 **Prices** FF **Evening meal** by request **Credit Cards** no
Children yes **Closed** never **Languages** English

Suresnes, W of Paris

39 rue Emile Duclaux

Mme Josepha Martins' small flat in an apartment block some 15 minutes from the middle of Paris is useful for the cost-conscious. The two bedrooms are plain and simple, nothing more. Near Bois de Boulogne, public transport. Telephone ahead of time.
Directions 8 km W of Paris in suburb of Suresnes. Telephone for directions. Nearest railway station: Puteaux (750 m).

❖ 39 rue Emile Duclaux, 92150 Suresnes **Tel** 1 47 72 22 27
Rooms 2 **Prices** FF **Evening meal** by request **Credit Cards** no
Children yes **Closed** never **Languages** French only

Le Vésinet, W of Paris

33 allée de la Meute

Le Vésinet, in a loop of the River Seine, was France's first planned garden suburb and is still quiet and leafy. M and Mme René Marabelle have an attractive turn-of-the-century house with one comfortable bedroom for guests.
Directions 15 km W of Paris. Take N 186 to Le Vésinet. Near Stade des Merlettes (stadium). Telephone for directions.

❖ 33 allée de la Meute, 78110 Le Vésinet **Tel** 1 30 71 45 60
Rooms 1 **Prices** FF **Evening meal** by request **Credit Cards** no
Children yes **Closed** never **Languages** English, German, Italian

---

Villepreux, W of Versailles

Château de Villepreux

Mme de Pompadour and Chateaubriand were guests in the 18thC ancestral home of the Comtesse de St-Seine. The glamour seems worn now and prices are exorbitant considering some rooms share WC. Next to St-Nom-la-Bretèche golf course.
Directions 10 km W of Versailles. Take D 11, right on D 98 in Villepreux. Signposted on right beyond town.

❖ 78450 Villepreux **Tel** 1 30 80 50 00 **Fax** 1 30 56 12 12 **Rooms** 11
Prices FFFF **Evening meal** by request **Credit Cards** MC V
Children yes **Closed** never **Languages** English

Eguisheim, SW of Colmar

3 rue des Fleurs

Christiane Gaschy is upgrading the bathrooms in her modern suburban villa where she has been taking guests for a decade.
Bedrooms in the lofted roof are plain; breakfast is served in the
conservatory; the garden is small. Children can play table tennis.
Directions 5 km SW of Colmar, just off N 83. Ask for directions in
the town.

❖ 3 rue des Fleurs, 68420 Eguisheim **Tel** 89 23 69 09 **Rooms** 3
Prices FF **Evening meal** no **Credit Cards** no **Children** yes
Closed never **Languages** German, some English

Eguisheim, SW of Colmar

3 rue du Riesling

Eguisheim, with its medieval houses, deserves a better place to
stay. Although Mme Hertz-Meyer renovated what was a ruined
house in 1957, it desperately needs another facelift now. The new
blue bedroom is the only one we would book into.
Directions 5 km SW of Colmar, just off N 83. Inside medieval walls.
Ask for directions.

❖ 3 rue du Riesling, 68420 Eguisheim **Tel** 89 23 67 74 **Fax** 89 23
99 23 **Rooms** 4 **Prices** FF **Evening meal** no **Credit Cards** no
Children no **Closed** never **Languages** German, some English

---

L'Epine-aux-Bois, W of Montmirail

Les Patrus

The low stone buildings surrounding a traditional farmyard have
been transformed into a busy hive of activity. Some guests play
bridge or practise music, others ride horses, walk or bicycle on the
estate. Mary-Ann Royol's regional cooking is well-priced.
Directions 10 km W of Montmirail. Take D 933. Left at la Haute-
Epine on D 863. Signposted on right after 500 m.

❖ L'Epine-aux-Bois, 02540 Viels-Maisons **Tel** 23 69 85 85 **Fax** 23 69
98 49 **Rooms** 5 **Prices** FF **Evening meal** by request **Credit Cards** V
Children yes **Closed** never **Languages** English, German

Estissac, W of Troyes

Moulin d'Eguebaude

Above a tumbling, rocky stream, an 18thC half-timber and brick
water-mill has been transformed into a fine spot to stay, with attractive bedrooms. Madame Mesley's evening meals are a bargain.
Guests can even fish for trout in the Vanne river.
Directions 22 km W of Troyes. Take N 60 to Estissac. At T-junction
in town, turn left, then right. At end of lane.

❖ 10190 Estissac **Tel** 25 40 42 18 **Fax** 25 29 30 30 **Rooms** 5
Prices FF **Evening meal** by request **Credit Cards** no **Children** yes
Closed never **Languages** French only

Herbéviller, SW of Blâmont

7 Route Nationale

A tidy herbaceous border greets motorists at this convenient overnight stop on the main road. Brigitte Brégeard offers a well-prepared, well-priced evening meal as well as picnics for hikers. One bedroom in this pink stone farmhouse opens on to the garden.
Directions 9 km SW of Blâmont. The house is on the N 4 in the middle of Herbéviller.

❖ 54450 Herbéviller **Tel** 83 72 24 73 **Rooms** 2 **Prices** FF
Evening meal by request **Credit Cards** no **Children** yes
Closed never **Languages** English, German

Mittelbergheim, N of Sélestat

La Tulipe

The Dolders' modern villa is opposite a vineyard in a classic Alsatian wine village. Spacious and comfortable, bedrooms are like apartments and are regularly rented by families for a week at a time. There is a washing machine, outdoor grill, bicycle hire.
Directions 14 km N of Sélestat. Take N 422; turn left at St-Pierre. Follow signs after 2 km.

❖ 15 Chemin de Holzweg, 67140 Mittelbergheim **Tel** 88 08 15 23
Rooms 5 **Prices** FF **Evening meal** by request **Credit Cards** no
Children yes **Closed** never **Languages** German

Vic-sur-Aisne, W of Soissons

Domaine des Jeanne

On the banks of the Aisne river, Anne and Jean Martner have worked hard to create a practical place for families to enjoy themselves: tennis and table tennis, swimming-pool and fishing are all on offer on the estate. Bedrooms overlook the park.
Directions 16 km W of Soissons. Take N 31. Signposted in town. Located off main square in rue Dubarle.

❖ rue Dubarle, 02290 Vic-sur-Aisne **Tel and Fax** 23 55 57 33
Rooms 5 **Prices** FFF **Evening meal** by request **Credit Cards** MC V
Children yes **Closed** never **Languages** English

Villers-Agron, SW of Reims

La Ferme du Château

Part 13thC fortress, part farmhouse, this was restored to create a home that is informal and seemingly full of children. Christine Ferry's well-priced dinners are praised. Tennis-court.
Directions 30 km SW of Reims. Take A 4 Dormans exit. Follow signs for Fère-en-Tardenois via D 2. House is next to Golf de Champagne course.

❖ 02130 Villers-Agron **Tel** 23 71 60 67 **Fax** 23 69 36 54 **Rooms** 4
Prices FFF **Evening meal** by request **Credit Cards** no **Children** yes
Closed never **Languages** English, German

Azay-le-Rideau

Manoir de la Remonière

Mme Pecas renovated her attractive manor house, mixing old with new and adding a sauna. She is not always at home, so her house-keeper takes over, making this quite business-like. Expensive, but stunning views of Azay-le-Rideau's château.
Directions cross bridge over Indre river to la Chapelle-St-Blaise. Turn left on D 17; house is on left, facing château.

❖ Cheillé, 37190 Azay-le-Rideau **Tel** 47 45 24 88 **Rooms** 5
Prices FFFF **Evening meal** by request **Credit Cards** no **Children** yes
Closed weekdays Nov to Easter **Languages** English, Italian

Bersac-sur-Rivalier, NE of Limoges

Domaine du Noyer

The Masdoumier's stone home is deep in the country. Families enjoy the swimming-pool, gymnasium and comfortable bedrooms up spiral stairs. Jean is a sculptor, Anna a homoeopathist. Dinners include local pork, rabbit, orchard fruits. Value for money.
Directions 42 km NE of Limoges. N 20 to Chanteloube; right on D 28, via Bersac. After railway bridge, left on D 28a. Signs.

❖ 87370 Bersac-sur-Rivalier **Tel** 55 71 59 54 **Rooms** 4 **Prices** FF
Evening meal by request **Credit Cards** no **Children** yes
Closed never **Languages** English

Bournand, SW of Chinon

Château de Bournand

Partly 12thC, but mainly 17thC, the informality of Christian Laurens' château is reflected in the large, but rustic, bedrooms. These have exposed beams, tiled floors, some old furniture plus satellite television, telephones. Set in a well-tended park.
Directions 18 km SW of Chinon. Head for Loudun and D 759, but quickly bear right on D 24, D 39 to Bournand. Signposted.

❖ 86120 Bournand **Tel** 49 98 77 82 **Fax** 49 98 97 30 **Rooms** 3
Prices FFF **Evening meal** by request **Credit Cards** no **Children** yes
Closed never; telephone in winter **Languages** English, Spanish, Italian, Japanese

---

Bourré, SW of Blois

Manoir de la Salle

The terraced gardens overlooking the Cher are sunny enough to grow orange trees. The Boussards' elegant 18thC mansion is a gen-teel, if expensive, base for seeing the Loire châteaux. Antiques are in bedrooms. Tennis-court and fishing on the estate.
Directions 37 km SW of Blois. Take D 751, D 764 to Montrichard, left on D 176 along river. House on left past Bourré.

❖ 69 route de Vierzon, 41400 Bourré **Tel** 54 32 73 54 **Rooms** 4
Prices FFFF **Evening meal** no **Credit Cards** V **Children** yes
Closed never **Languages** English, Spanish

Buzançais, NW of Châteauroux

Château de Bois-Renault

A forest of oak trees must have been felled to panel the interior of this Renaissance-style, 19thC mansion. The dark, carved wood, hung with tapestries, can be quite gloomy but Mme du Manoir is a lively hostess. Swimming-pool in the grounds.
Directions 28 km NW of Châteauroux. N 143 into Buzançais; right on D 926. House on right, just outside Buzançais.

❖ 36500 Buzançais **Tel** 54 84 03 01 **Fax** 54 84 10 57 **Rooms** 5 **Prices** FFF **Evening meal** by request **Credit Cards** AE V **Children** yes **Closed** mid-Dec to Jan **Languages** English

---

Châteauneuf-la-Forêt, SE of Limoges

La Croix du Reh

Tea and cakes are a bonus in the 17thC house that has been restored with care by Scots Elizabeth and Patrick McLaughlin. The gardens are a delight; evening meals are a treat, with Scottish, Swiss and international dishes. Value for money.
Directions 35 km SE of Limoges. Take D 979. Châteauneuf-la-Forêt is signposted on right.

❖ rue Amédée Tarrade, 87130 Châteauneuf-la-Forêt **Tel** 55 69 75 37 **Fax** 55 69 75 38 **Rooms** 5 **Prices** FF **Evening meal** by request **Credit Cards** V **Children** yes **Closed** never **Languages** English

---

Chauvigny, E of Poitiers

La Chantellerie

The Gaydon family run an old-fashioned, basic but clean place to stay in the middle of an attractive medieval town, not far from Futuroscope. Two bedrooms are in a separate building and share facilities. Secure, private parking. A terrace garden overlooks the town.
Directions 18 km E of Poitiers. In the middle of Chauvigny.

❖ 6 rue St-Pierre, 86300 Chauvigny **Tel** 49 46 32 99 **Rooms** 3 **Prices** FF **Evening meal** no **Credit Cards** no **Children** yes **Closed** never; telephone in winter **Languages** French only

---

Isle, SW of Limoges

Verthamont

This modern, purpose-built house overlooking the Vienne river lacks privacy but is a useful overnight stop. Enthusiastic hosts Edith and Jean-François Brunier offer a bargain evening meal using their own organic vegetables. Swimming-pool.
Directions 8 km SW of Limoges. Take N 21. Turn right after the hamlet of Bas-Verthamont. House is 600 m, signposted.

❖ Pic de l'Aiguille, 87110 Isle **Tel** 55 36 12 89 **Rooms** 3 **Prices** FF **Evening meal** by request **Credit Cards** no **Children** yes **Closed** never **Languages** English, German

===

La Jaille-Yvon, NW of Angers

Château du Plessis-Anjou

The Mayenne river valley is pretty and the creeper-covered 16th-18thC château, set in a vast park, is equally attractive. Simone and Paul Benoist welcome guests with a glass of wine but dinner is expensive. Recommendation: go out to a local restaurant.
Directions 35 km NW of Angers. N 162 through le Lion d'Angers; right on D 189 to La Jaille-Yvon. House signposted on right.

❖ 49220 La Jaille-Yvon **Tel** 41 95 12 75 **Fax** 41 95 14 41 **Rooms** 8 **Prices** FFFF **Evening meal** by request **Credit Cards** MC V **Children** yes **Closed** Nov to Feb **Languages** English, Spanish

===

Jazeneuil, SW of Poitiers

Château de la Barre

Set in a spacious, wooded park, Michel Lorphelin's elegant, late-18thC, Directoire-style home has huge fireplaces and painted ceilings. Bedrooms have some antiques. Friendly ambience. Guests may fish in the Vonne river.
Directions 25 km SW of Poitiers. N 11 to Coulombiers; right on D 95; right before Jazeneuil for Villiers. House on left before A 10.

❖ 86600 Jazeneuil **Tel** 49 53 50 46 **Rooms** 2 **Prices** FFF **Evening meal** by request **Credit Cards** V **Children** yes **Closed** Oct to May **Languages** some English, German

===

Jazeneuil, SW of Poitiers

Les Ruffinières

Denyse Foucault has an attractive house surrounded by trees and covered in wistaria and creeper. The approach is lined with red roses; the conservatory at the front overlooks the garden. The bedrooms are well-furnished. 33 km from Futuroscope.
Directions 25 km SW of Poitiers. N 11 to Coulombiers; right on D 95 for Jazeneuil. Signposted on left on edge of Jazeneuil.

❖ 86600 Jazeneuil **Tel** 49 53 55 19 **Rooms** 5 **Prices** FF **Evening meal** by request **Credit Cards** no **Children** yes **Closed** mid-Nov to mid-March **Languages** some English

===

Marennes, SW of Rochefort

La Menardière

In this village famous for its oysters, Jean Ferchaud has a pleasant, ivy-clad house. Driving into the courtyard, guests are greeted by a display of pink and red geraniums. Both bedrooms have bathrooms but share WC. Useful overnight stop.
Directions 24 km SW of Rochefort. Ask for rue des Lilas in Marennes village.

❖ 5 rue des Lilas, 17320 Marennes **Tel** 46 85 41 77 **Rooms** 2 **Prices** FF **Evening meal** no **Credit Cards** no **Children** yes **Closed** never **Languages** French only

---

Moreilles, W of Fontenay-le-Comte

Le Château

Cardinal Richelieu once headed the abbey here. Now Danielle Renard offers popular, if expensive, evening meals in her creeper-covered house. Comfortable bedrooms have telephones; some have traffic noise. Bicycles available; swimming-pool.

Directions 30 km W of Fontenay-le-Comte. Take D 949 to Quatre-Chemins. Left on N 137. House on left beyond Moreilles.

❖ 85450 Moreilles **Tel** 51 56 17 56 **Fax** 51 56 30 30 **Rooms** 6
Prices FFFF **Evening meal** by request **Credit Cards** no
Children yes **Closed** never; telephone in winter
Languages English

Mosnes, E of Tours

Château de la Barre

Guests praise Patricia Marlière's cooking, including her home-made bread at breakfast. Her 150-year-old château on the Loire River has one guest bedroom in the house, a suite and two more rooms in converted outbuildings. Attractive winter break prices.

Directions 35 km E of Tours. Take D 751 along Loire for Mosnes. Château on right, 1 km before village.

❖ 37530 Mosnes **Tel** 47 57 33 40 **Rooms** 4 **Prices** FFF
Evening Meal by request **Credit Cards** no **Children** yes
Closed never **Languages** English

Mosnes, E of Tours

Les Hauts-Noyers

With its sloping, tiled roof and white walls, the Saltrons' restored 100-year-old farmhouse is a pretty base to explore the Loire valley. Vineyards nearby. The Blue bedroom is on the ground floor. Bicycles may be borrowed. Self-catering available in winter.

Directions 35 km E of Tours. Take D 751 along Loire; in Mosnes, on D 123 for 2 km. Signposted in Les Hauts-Noyers.

❖ 37530 Mosnes **Tel** 47 57 19 73 **Fax** 47 48 37 13 **Rooms** 2
Prices FF **Evening meal** no **Credit Cards** no **Children** yes
Closed never **Languages** French only

Pageas, SW of Limoges

Les Ourgeaux

Another British enterprise: John Higham and Vanessa McKeand converted a stone farmhouse and now have a tiny restaurant with room for ten plus three bedrooms. With a neat lawn and pond, it is worth more than an overnight stop.

Directions 35 km SW of Limoges. N 21 past Pageas to Châlus; right on D 901. After 2.5 km, follow signs on right; house 700 m.

❖ 87230 Pageas **Tel** 55 78 50 97 **Fax** 55 78 54 76 **Rooms** 3
Prices FFF **Evening meal** no by request **Credit Cards** MC V
Children yes **Closed** never **Languages** English

Château de Vaumoret

Odile Vaucamp has renovated a wing of her 17thC château over-looking a courtyard. Guests use a sitting-room with stereo, television; also a kitchen to prepare picnics and light meals. Fine for families. Near Futuróscope. Restaurants in Poitiers.
Directions Due E of Poitiers, just beyond city off D 6. Signposted on left after 6 km.

❖ Le Breuil-Mingot, 86000 Poitiers **Tel** 49 61 32 11 **Fax** 49 01 04 54 **Rooms** 3 **Prices** FFF **Evening meal** no **Credit Cards** no **Children** yes **Closed** Nov to Easter; telephone in winter **Languages** English

Château de la Roche du Maine

An impressive castle with turrets and towers, rescued and modernised by M and Mme Jacques Neveu at great expense. Antique furniture throughout. Two luxurious bedrooms in the château; four in outbuildings. Heated indoor swimming-pool.
Directions 10 km SW of Richelieu. Take D 749; bear right on D 22, D 46. Signposted on left, before Prinçay.

❖ 86420 Prinçay **Tel** 49 22 84 09 **Fax** 49 22 89 57 **Rooms** 6 **Prices** FFFF **Evening meal** by request **Credit Cards** MC V **Children** over 10 **Closed** never; telephone in winter **Languages** English

1 rue Jarry

Mme Leplatre takes care over breakfast, served in the sunroom of her handsome 17thC town house. Family heirlooms fill bedrooms in the main house, once part of a convent. She often walks with guests through the attractive town, explaining the history.
Directions in town, corner of rue Jarry and place des Religieuses.

❖ 1 rue Jarry, 37120 Richelieu **Tel** 47 58 10 42 **Rooms** 4 **Prices** FF **Evening meal** no **Credit Cards** no **Children** yes **Closed** never **Languages** French only

Chez Jaubert

In the Limoges hills, an artistic couple have converted an old stone house into a home. Michel Jaubert teaches painting and sculpting but also loves classic sports cars. Bedrooms, in a separate building, are new and practical. Restaurants in Eymoutiers.
Directions 45 km SE of Limoges. Take D 979 to Eymoutiers; right on D 30. At La Roche, signposted on left.

❖ La Roche, 87120 Eymoutiers **Tel** 55 69 61 88 **Fax** 55 69 12 36 **Rooms** 3 **Prices** FF **Evening meal** no **Credit Cards** no **Children** yes **Closed** never **Languages** English, German

---

Château de Montgouverne

Handy for Vouvray's vineyards and Tours, the Desvignes' 18thC country house is in parkland with a heated swimming-pool. Bedrooms are comfortable, with telephone and television. Dinner seems expensive, but the price includes drinks.
Directions 4 km NE of Tours. Take N 152 for Vouvray. Turn left towards St-Georges. Château on right before Rochecorbon.

❖ 37210 Rochecorbon **Tel** 47 52 84 59 **Fax** 47 52 84 61 **Rooms** 6
Prices FFFF **Evening meal** by request **Credit Cards** V **Children** yes
Closed never **Languages** English

Le Castel du Verger

An impressive 15thC fortified manor, with castellated tower and an 18thC chapel with painted statues. Guests appreciate the comfortable bedrooms, heated swimming-pool, and gardens. Value for money, especially for dinner, bed-and-breakfast.
Directions 30 km NW of La Roche-sur-Yon. Take D 948. House signposted at the entrance to St-Christophe-du-Ligneron.

❖ 85670 St-Christophe-du-Ligneron **Tel** 51 93 04 14 **Rooms** 6
Prices FFF **Evening meal** by request **Credit Cards** no **Children** yes
Closed never **Languages** English

Manoir de Ponsay

A business-like operation in a severe-looking 15thC house where King Louis XI slept and the de Ponsay family has lived for 350 years. Dinner looks expensive but includes aperitifs, wines.
Directions 38 km E of La-Roche-sur-Yon. Take D 948, D 949b to Chantonnay, then D 960b to Puybelliard. Right for St-Mars-des-Prés. Signposted on left.

❖ St-Mars-des-Prés, 85110 Chantonnay **Tel** 51 46 96 71
Fax 51 46 80 07 **Rooms** 8 **Prices** FFFF **Evening meal** by request
Credit Cards AE **Children** yes **Closed** never; telephone in winter
Languages English, German

Château de Thaumiers

Well off the tourist beat, the Vicomte and Vicomtesse de Bonneval own a pretty, pale stone, L-shaped château. This is expensive, but regulars feel it is worth it for the formal lake, swimming-pool, tennis-court and golf practice area.
Directions 35 km SE of Bourges. Take N 76; bear right on D 953 via Dun-sur-Auron. Sign for château on right in Thaumiers.

❖ Thaumiers, 18210 Charenton-sur-Cher **Tel** 48 61 81 62 **Fax** 48 61 81 82 **Rooms** 9 **Prices** FFFF **Evening meal** by request
Credit Cards V **Children** yes **Closed** never **Languages** English

Autrans, W of Grenoble
Le Tracollet

Surrounded by old cartwheels and ploughs, Alain and Marie Arnaud's renovated farmhouse is 1.5 km outside the small ski resort of Autrans. Popular with the hiker/cross-country skier crowd. Breakfast is served until 11am; hearty dinners.
Directions 30 km W of Grenoble. Take N 532, D 531, then turn right on D 106 to Autrans. House is on way to Stade de Neige.

❖ Eybertière, 38880 Autrans **Tel** 76 95 37 23 **Rooms** 5 **Prices** FF **Evening meal** by request **Credit Cards** no **Children** yes **Closed** never **Languages** French only

Baume-les-Messieurs, NE of Lons-le-Saunier
L'Abbaye

This massive stone house was originally a famous abbey with a history dating back 1,000 years. All rooms are vast and the two echoing bedrooms were once the Abbot's chambers. Best in warm weather. Restaurants one minute away.
Directions 20 km NE of Lons-le-Saunier. Take N 83 to St-Germain. Right on D 120, D 70 to Baume-les-Messieurs.

❖ 39210 Baume-les-Messieurs **Tel** 84 44 64 47 **Rooms** 2 **Prices** FF **Evening meal** no **Credit Cards** no **Children** yes **Closed** mid-Oct to April **Languages** English

Chamagnieu, SE of Lyon
Le Chevallet

A useful if expensive overnight stay near Lyon-Satolas airport. Hélène Rousset is proud of her Mâcon and Lyon-style dishes. Old-fashioned rooms. Swimming-pool, tennis-court. Hard to find.
Directions 28 km SE of Lyon. Take A 43; take Isle d'Abeau Ouest exit. Follow D 75 towards Crémieu. At Chamagnieu traffic-lights, turn right and left; right and left again. House on left.

❖ 38460 Chamagnieu **Tel** 74 90 31 03 **Fax** 74 90 20 54 **Rooms** 2 **Prices** FFF **Evening meal** by request **Credit Cards** no **Children** yes **Closed** never **Languages** French only

Chasselay, N of St-Marcellin
La Bourrelière

Christian Beaucourt runs a popular *ferme-auberge* in the walnut trees on the edge of the village. In 1993 he opened six rooms for guests: beds and bathrooms are new, but the look is dull. Families like the rural simplicity, handy restaurant, splendid views.
Directions 12 km N of St-Marcellin. Take D 518 to village.

❖ Auberge de Campagne, 38470 Chasselay **Tel** 76 64 21 03 **Fax** 76 64 25 97 **Rooms** 6 **Prices** FF **Evening meal** restaurant **Credit Cards** AE MC V **Children** yes **Closed** never **Languages** English, German, Italian, Portuguese

---

Chevagny-les-Chevrières, W of Mâcon

Le Bourg

'France without the frills' is the verdict on this 17thC sandstone farmhouse in a pretty Mâconnais wine village. Mme Marin offers a glass of her own wine on arrival. In a converted farm building, modern bedrooms have garish colours. Restaurant across street.
Directions 4 km W of Mâcon. Take N 79, then right on D 194 to village. Well-signposted.

❖ 71960 Chevagny-les-Chevrières **Tel** 85 34 78 60 **Rooms** 3
Prices FF **Evening meal** no **Credit Cards** no **Children** yes
Closed never **Languages** some English

Chorey-lès-Beaune, N of Beaune

15 rue d'Aloxe-Corton

Henri and Marie-Claire Deschamps are a welcoming couple. Their modern home, on the edge of the village and next to vineyards, is a useful overnight stop. Tidy but plain, the simply furnished bedrooms have small refrigerators and telephones.
Directions 3 km N of Beaune. Take N 74 for Nuits-St-Georges. Turn right for Chorey and follow signs.

❖ 15 rue d'Aloxe-Corton, 21200 Chorey-lès-Beaune **Tel** 80 24 08 13
Fax 80 24 08 01 **Rooms** 6 **Prices** FF **Evening meal** no **Credit Cards** no **Children** yes **Closed** Dec, Jan **Languages** French only

---

Cottance, NE of Feurs

Le Bois Prieur

In the upper Loire valley, this former farmhouse is now a luxurious resort-style getaway with a tennis-court and swimming-pool. Updated bedrooms have telephones, television. Hélène Bonnard's evening meals are candle-lit, by a log fire. Expensive.
Directions 13 km NE of Feurs. Take D 89, then D 60 for Panissières. Left on D 113. Signposted 3km before Cottance.

❖ 42360 Cottance **Tel** 77 28 06 69 **Fax** 77 28 00 55 **Rooms** 5
Prices FFFF **Evening meal** by request **Credit Cards** MC V
Children yes **Closed** mid-Oct to mid-April **Languages** English

---

Donzy, E of Cosne-sur-Loire

Jardins de Belle Rive

Josette and Bernard Juste have a pleasant home among willow trees. Guests stay in the delightful cottage next door: three comfortable bedrooms plus a sitting-room, small kitchen, fireplace. Swimming-pool. Fly-fishing 200 m. Book well in advance.
Directions 18 km E of Cosne-sur-Loire. Take D 33 to Donzy. Follow signs to Bagnaux along Talvane river. Signposted.

❖ Bagnaux, 58220 Donzy **Tel** 86 39 42 18 **Rooms** 3 **Prices** FF
Evening meal no **Credit Cards** no **Children** yes **Closed** never
Languages English

Epenoux, N of Vesoul

Château d'Epenoux

Not far from the Swiss and German borders, the Vosges mountains and Saône valley. A 17thC chapel is in the quiet grounds of Germaine Gauthier's pretty 18thC château. Bedrooms are comfortable. Fair prices for half-board.
Directions 5 km N of Vesoul. Take D 10 to Epenoux. Signposted.

❖ route de St-Loup, Epenoux, 70000 Vesoul **Tel** 84 75 19 60
Rooms 5 **Prices** FF **Evening meal** by request **Credit Cards** AE
Children yes **Closed** never **Languages** English

Escolives-Ste-Camille, S of Auxerre

Château d'Escolives

With old arches, a covered staircase, tower and courtyard, this could be a setting for a medieval children's story. Gérard Borgnat is a wine producer whose vast cellars are full of oak barrels. Régine's cooking is popular. Attractively priced.
Directions 10 km S of Auxerre. Take D 239, then D 563 to village. Near church.

❖ 89290 Escolives-Ste-Camille **Tel** 86 53 35 28 **Fax** 86 53 65 00
Rooms 5 **Prices** FF **Evening meal** by request **Credit Cards** MC V
Children yes **Closed** never **Languages** English, German

Gillonnay, E of la Côte-St-André

La Ferme des Collines

Flowers at the door, logs piled by a wall and dried flowers in baskets make Jean-Marc and Marie Meyer's green and yellow wooden farmhouse attractive. With lawns and rose-covered pergola, it has the rural peace many seek. Pretty bedrooms.
Directions 2 km E of la Côte-St-André. Turn off D 73 and follow signs up long winding road above Gillonnay.

❖ Hameau Notre-Dame, 38260 Gillonnay **Tel** 74 20 27 93
Rooms 2 **Prices** FF **Evening meal** no **Credit Cards** no **Children** yes
Closed never **Languages** English, Italian

La Guiche, S of Montceau-les-Mines

Château de Dravert

Bernard Monnet's L-shaped country house, built on magnificent 12thC wine cellars, is like a luxury hotel: Jacuzzis in bathrooms, embroidered bed-linen, fabric-covered walls and an indoor heated swimming-pool. Expensive, especially with a candle-lit dinner.
Directions 25 km S of Montceau-les-Mines. Take D 980; turn right on D 33; D 27 to La Guiche. Signposted.

❖ 71220 La Guiche **Tel** 85 24 67 38 **Fax** 85 24 69 69 **Rooms** 4
Prices FFFF **Evening meal** by request **Credit Cards** V **Children** yes
Closed mid-Nov to Easter **Languages** English

Lucenay, NW of Lyon

La Fontaine

Right on the main road, but hidden behind a high hedge, Jacques and Marie-Claude Torret's home is in a Beaujolais vineyard. The outside is attractive, the interior is dull. The bedroom has its own entrance. The main advantage is the swimming-pool.
Directions 25 km NW of Lyon. Take N 6, then D 485 to Civrieux d'Azergues. Take D 30 to Lucenay. Follow signs.

❖ 69480 Lucenay **Tel** 74 67 05 42 **Rooms** 1 **Prices** FF **Evening meal** no **Credit Cards** no **Children** yes **Closed** Sept, Oct; weekdays in winter **Languages** French only

---

Meursault, S of Beaune

2 rue de la Velle

Like the local Burgundy wines, Alain Zorninger's 17thC wine-grower's mansion is a special but expensive experience. Gourmet dinners include wines from the 15thC cellars. The two suites have antiques, the grand bathrooms boast Jacuzzis.
Directions 7 km S of Beaune. N 74; right at the Hôpital de Meursault. After 1 km, left to St-Aubin; rue de la Velle 500 m beyond.

❖ 2 rue de la Velle, 21190 Meursault **Tel** 80 21 65 69 **Fax** 1 42 71 08 66 **Rooms** 2 **Prices** FFFF **Evening meal** by request **Credit Cards** no **Children** no **Closed** Dec to Easter **Languages** English

---

Morey-St-Denis, S of Dijon

34 route des Grands Crus

Modest and quiet, Jean-Pierre Duprey-Gautier is a wine grower, as the wooden barrel by the door of his big, old ivy-clad house indicates. Three bedrooms share a bath and shower, so this is no more than a useful base in Burgundy. Little interaction with host.
Directions 12 km S of Dijon. Take N 74 to Morey-St-Denis. House on main road in village.

❖ 34 route des Grands Crus, 21220 Morey-St-Denis **Tel** 80 51 82 88 **Rooms** 5 **Prices** FF **Evening meal** no **Credit Cards** no **Children** yes **Closed** Jan, Feb **Languages** French only

---

Noiron-sous-Gevrey, S of Dijon

7 route de Dijon

Farmer's wife Nicole Maret has just redecorated two bedrooms and upgraded their bathrooms, so her family home is a useful if simple address near Burgundy's famous vineyards. Crisp bed-linen and curtains, fluffy towels. Nicole also paints and sculpts.
Directions 15 km S of Dijon. Take D 966. Farm is on main road in Noiron, well-signposted.

❖ 7 route de Dijon, 21910 Noiron-sous-Gevrey **Tel** 80 36 64 17 **Rooms** 2 **Prices** FF **Evening meal** no **Credit Cards** no **Children** yes **Closed** never **Languages** French only

Le Charveyron

A useful place to stay the night, but not our idea of a bed-and-breakfast, since the Laracine family don't live on the premises and breakfast is taken at their excellent *ferme-auberge* a 3 min walk away. Snug bedrooms with modern bathrooms. Skiing.
Directions 20 km NW of Belley. Follow D 32 mountain road through Contrevoz to Ordonnaz. Enquire at ferme-auberge.

❖ 01510 Ordonnaz **Tel** 74 40 90 20 **Rooms** 3 **Prices** FF
Evening meal no **Credit Cards** no **Children** yes **Closed** Dec
Languages French only

La Coudre

The Lusardis' remote, renovated farmhouse has quality furniture and fabrics and their pottery workshop. Dinner is somewhat expensive, but well-presented and prepared. Special rates for children.
Directions 48 km NW of Auxerre. Take D 965 to Toucy; right on D 955; fork left on D 3, Left at Sommecaise on D 57. House 1 km before Perreux.

❖ 89120 Perreux **Tel** 86 91 61 42 **Rooms** 3 **Prices** FFF
Evening meal by request **Credit Cards** V **Children** yes **Closed** never
Languages English

La Rêverie

Maoudo and Paul Lapeyrade own the art gallery in this late 19thC town house which they renovated in 1988. Bedrooms are comfortable but the decoration may be too intense for some: red velvet and chandeliers, statuettes and modern art.
Directions 15 km S of Cosne-sur-Loire. Take N 7. Located in the middle of the village.

❖ 6 rue Joyeuse, 58150 Pouilly-sur-Loire **Tel** 86 39 07 87 **Rooms** 5
Prices FFF **Evening meal** no **Credit Cards** no **Children** yes
Closed never **Languages** English

Manoir de Tarperon

Antiques fill this plain château. The sitting-room is mainly Chinese. Portraits of Mme Soisick de Champsavin's ancestors cover walls. Bedrooms are in bold colours; bathrooms have whimsical artwork. Expensive but worthwhile evening meals.
Directions 28 km S of Châtillon-sur-Seine. Take N 71, D 32. At Cosne, bear left on D 954. Signposted on right.

❖ Quemigny-sur-Seine, 21510 Aignay-le-Duc **Tel** 80 93 83 74
Rooms 5 **Prices** FFF **Evening meal** by request **Credit Cards** no
Children yes **Closed** Nov to mid-March **Languages** English,
German

Les Roches de Condrieu, SW of Vienne

Le Pré Margot

Perched on a hillside with views over the Rhône valley. Maurice
and Martine Briot are a popular stopover on the way to the coast.
Guests enjoy large meals in the conservatory/dining-room.
Bedrooms have television, air-conditioning. Railway line nearby.
Directions 10 km SW of Vienne. D 4 on east bank of Rhône.
House signposted on left just before Les Roches de Condrieu.

❖ chemin de Pré-Margot, St-Prim, 38370 Les Roches de Condrieu
Tel 74 56 44 27 **Fax** 74 56 30 93 **Rooms** 5 **Prices** FF
Evening meal by request **Credit Cards** no **Children** yes
Closed Christmas **Languages** English, German

St-Aubin, NE of Paray-le-Monial

Château de Poujux

For lovers of thoroughbred racehorses, since the Céaly-Oberli family run a century-old stud farm. The interior does not fulfill the
promise of the outside of the 15thC château. Expensive. Some criticism of evening meals. Restaurant at Paray-le-Monial.
Directions 12 km NE of Paray-le-Monial. Take N 79, N 70. Right
on D 25 towards St-Aubin. House on left before village.

❖ St-Aubin-en-Charollais, 71430 Palinges **Tel** 85 70 43 64 **Rooms** 7
Prices FFF **Evening meal** by request **Credit Cards** no
Children yes **Closed** never **Languages** English, German

St-Marcellin-en-Forez, NW of St-Etienne

40 route de St-Bonnet-le-Château

A useful overnight stop if you have to leave the A 72 motorway
near St-Etienne. Roland Malcles has four bedrooms in a separate
stone house in the garden. Although there is a swimming-pool and
tennis-court, this is next to a busy road. Plain bedrooms.
Directions 26 km NW of St-Etienne. Take D 8 via St-Rambert; turn
left on to D 498. House is on main road in St-Marcellin.

❖ 40 route de St-Bonnet-le-Château, 42680 St-Marcellin-en-Forez
Tel 77 52 89 63 **Rooms** 4 **Prices** FF **Evening meal** no
Credit Cards no **Children** yes **Closed** never **Languages** French only

---

Villié-Morgon, S of Mâcon

La Javernière

François Roux runs a business-like operation in the world-famous
Beaujolais vineyards. Lines of vines ambush the cream-coloured
house on all sides. Bedrooms are well-furnished, with quality furniture and fabrics. Expensive: breakfast is extra.
Directions 25 km S of Mâcon. A 6 to Belleville exit; D 37 to Cercié;
right on D 68 through Morgon. Sign 600 m on right.

❖ 69910 Villié-Morgon **Tel** 74 04 22 71 **Fax** 74 69 14 44 **Rooms** 9
Prices FFFF **Evening meal** no **Credit Cards** AE V
Children yes **Closed** Dec **Languages** French only

Avensac, SW of Montauban

La Chavinière

The owners of this luxurious 18thC country house offer health and fitness courses as well as meals of roast lamb or honey-roasted duck. Thierry and Yveline Morel-Nomblot also love golf, gardening and antiques. Swimming-pool and lake on estate.
Directions 40 km SW of Montauban. Take D 928 via Montech, Beaumont-de-Lomagne. 2 km after Gimat, signposted on right.

❖ 32120 Avensac **Tel** 62 65 03 43 **Fax** 62 65 03 23 **Rooms** 4 **Prices** FFF **Evening meal** by request **Credit Cards** no **Children** yes **Closed** never; telephone in advance **Languages** English, Spanish

---

Bassignac-le-Bas, SW of Argentat

Château de Chauvac

Children enjoy staying at this 500-year-old fortified stone manor house, with turrets and look-out points over the Dordogne River. Owner André Lavergne is enthusiastic. There is a pretty garden plus a large swimming-pool. Restaurant in Beaulieu (6 km).
Directions 15 km SW of Argentat. Take D 12; cross bridge at Brivezac to Bassignac. Signposted before Château du Doux.

❖ route d'Aurillac, 19430 Bassignac-le-Bas **Tel** 55 91 07 22 **Fax** 55 91 00 04 **Rooms** 4 **Prices** FF **Evening meal** no **Credit Cards** no **Children** yes **Closed** Oct to March **Languages** German

---

La Bastide-de-Sérou, NW of Foix

Fittes

Privacy here is assured since the only guest bedroom even has its own small sitting-room. Third bed available. Claude Benoît's 300-year-old château is outside the attractive village where there is a tennis-court and restaurant. Useful for overnight stay.
Directions 17 km NW of Foix. Take D 117. On leaving La Bastide-de-Sérou, take first left, second right.

❖ 09240 La Bastide-de-Sérou **Tel** 61 64 51 71 **Rooms** 1 **Prices** FF **Evening meal** no **Credit Cards** V **Children** yes **Closed** never **Languages** French only

---

Beaulieu-sur-Dordogne, SW of Argentat

11 rue de la Gendarmerie

This Spanish Colonial house, with patio and stone arches, was built by a soldier returning from Mexico in 1860. Imaginatively decorated by owner Christine Henriet, bedrooms are themed: a 1930s honeymoon suite, an Indian room. Bargain-priced dinners.
Directions 25 km SW of Argentat. Take D 12 along Dordogne valley. In middle of Beaulieu-sur-Dordogne.

❖ 11 rue de la Gendarmerie, 19120 Beaulieu-sur-Dordogne **Tel** 55 91 24 97 **Rooms** 6 **Prices** FF **Evening meal** by request **Credit Cards** no **Children** yes **Closed** Oct to April **Languages** French only

Bidart, S of Biarritz

Domaine de Bassilour

Set between the mountains and the sea, Charlotte and Jean-Marc Vachet's elegant 18thC mansion is in one of France's favourite resort areas. The atmosphere is relaxed, while Scandinavian ornaments are reminders that Charlotte is Swedish.
Directions 4 km S of Biarritz. Take D 255. Look for signs on right after Arbonne. Difficult to find.

❖ 64210 Bidart **Tel** 59 41 90 85 **Fax** 59 41 87 62 **Rooms** 6
Prices FF **Evening meal** no **Credit Cards** no **Children** yes
Closed never; telephone in winter **Languages** English, German, Portuguese, Swedish

Blaziert, SE of Condom

La Bajonne

Paintings by local artists are on the walls of this small, modernised farmhouse in a quiet, hilly part of Gers. Ingrid d'Aloia prepares *garbure* (vegetable soup), *thourin* (milk-and-onion soup), *magret de canard* and *poule au pot*. Value for money.
Directions 10 km SE of Condom. Take D 7; then turn right for Blaziert. Signposted.

❖ 32100 La Bajonne **Tel** 62 68 27 09 **Rooms** 4 **Prices** FF
Evening meal by request **Credit Cards** no **Children** yes
Closed never; telephone in advance **Languages** English, German

Calmont, SE of Toulouse

Château de Terraqueuse

A tall clock-tower marks the entrance to a large courtyard in this handsome Garonne château. Bedrooms are attractive, bathrooms modern, fresh flowers everywhere. Open only for a few weeks in summer. Prices are high. Restaurants are 10-15 km away.
Directions 45 km SE of Toulouse. Take N 20 to Les Baccarets; left on D 35. House (no sign) between Cintegabelle and Calmont.

❖ 31560 Calmont **Tel** 61 08 10 04 **Fax** 61 08 73 32 **Rooms** 3
Prices FFFF **Evening meal** no **Credit Cards** no **Children** yes
Closed Oct to mid-June **Languages** English

Camon, SE of Mirepoix

Château de Camon

Luxurious, expensive and in the foothills of the Pyrenees. The 16thC château, built on the ruins of a 10thC abbey, has a medieval interior with antiques, a gallery, monumental staircase. Hotel-like, with gourmet dinners. Swimming-pool, fly-fishing.
Directions 14 km SE of Mirepoix. Take D 625; left on D 7; continue right on D 7 to Camon. Well-signposted.

❖ Camon, 09500 Mirepoix **Tel** 61 68 14 05 **Fax** 61 68 81 56
Rooms 10 **Prices** FFFF **Evening meal** by request **Credit Cards** MC V **Children** yes **Closed** Dec to Feb **Languages** English

Chanteclair

This 19thC house has antiques and large comfortable bedrooms (though tartan bedspreads clash with floral curtains), plus a swimming-pool, swings and park. Unfortunately, the Larribeaus lack warmth and insist on a minimum of four for evening meals.
Directions 19 km N of Villeneuve-sur-Lot. Take N 21 to Cancon. Turn left on D 124 for Monbahus. House 300 m on left.

❖ 47290 Cancon **Tel** 53 01 63 34 **Fax** 53 41 13 44 **Rooms** 4 **Prices** FFF **Evening meal** by request **Credit Cards** no **Children** yes **Closed** never **Languages** Spanish

Château de Croisillat

Bernard Guérin is fighting an uphill battle to maintain this remote, ivy-covered castle, dating from the 14th to the 18thC and crammed with antiques. Useful if you have an ambition to stay in a château, but an expensive experience. Swimming-pool in grounds.
Directions 25 km SE of Toulouse. N 126 towards Castres. Right at Montauriol on D 1. 2 km past Caraman, on right.

❖ 31460 Caraman **Tel** 61 83 10 09 **Rooms** 5 **Prices** FFF **Evening meal** no **Credit Cards** no **Children** yes **Closed** mid-Nov to mid-March **Languages** English, German, Spanish

La Nougarède

Véronique Chiffoleau's old, converted house has lawns running down to the River Lot. Children splash around in the outdoor swimming-pool. The bedrooms are all on the ground floor. Evening meals could include rabbit with prunes.
Directions 10 km NW of Villeneuve-sur-Lot. In Casseneuil, before bridge, take D 225 on right. House signposted on left.

❖ Route de Castelmoron 47440 Casseneuil **Tel** 53 41 11 29 **Rooms** 5 **Prices** FFF **Evening meal** by request **Credit Cards** no **Children** yes **Closed** never **Languages** French only

Domaine de Carrat

These converted stables stand apart from the main house, so there is little contact with Mme Pery. Bedrooms have pretty matching curtains and bedspreads, modern bathrooms. No evening meal but guests may make their own in the kitchen. Value for money.
Directions 28 km NW of Bordeaux. Take D 1 to Castelnau and turn left on N 215 for Ste-Hélène. Look for signs.

❖ 33480 Castelnau-de-Médoc **Tel** 56 58 24 80 **Rooms** 3 **Prices** FF **Evening meal** no **Credit Cards** no **Children** yes **Closed** early July to early August **Languages** English, Spanish

---

Fajolles, N of Beaumont-de-Lomagne

Langans

One of only a dozen houses in the remote hamlet of Fajolles, this carefully restored 200-year-old stone house with its barrel-tiled roof and grey shutters hides a swimming-pool at the rear. Striking red geraniums and pink petunias complete the French look.

Directions 18 km N of Beaumont-de-Lomagne. Take D 928 NE to Larrazet, then D 25 W. Fajolles is signposted on right.

❖ Fajolles, 82210 St-Nicholas-de-la-Grave **Tel** 63 95 65 31
Fax 63 04 35 75 **Rooms** 5 **Prices** FF **Evening meal** by request
Credit Cards no **Children** yes **Closed** never **Languages** English

---

Gondrin, SW of Condom

Château de Polignac

Paul and Christine Sainsbury, a British couple, have worked hard to offer high standards of comfort in their small 19thC villa. Set in vineyards, it is totally secluded, deep in the Gers countryside. The well-priced evening meals are 'like a dinner party'.

Directions 16 km SW of Condom but not in Gondrin. Take D 931 to Mouchan; left on D 35; left after 4 km; follow signs for 2 km.

❖ 32330 Gondrin **Tel** 62 28 52 63 **Rooms** 4 **Prices** FFF
Evening meal by request **Credit Cards** no **Children** yes
Closed Christmas holidays **Languages** English

Laplume, SW of Agen

Cazeaux

Once part of the 1,000-year-old village church, this has spacious rooms. The Verguins are enthusiastic, helpful; their huge collection of model cars is on the galleried landing. Modern, clean bedrooms, but all share one bathroom and WC. Near Parc Walibi.

Directions 15 km SW of Agen. Take D 931 to Laplume. Near church.

❖ 47310 Laplume **Tel** 53 95 15 91 **Rooms** 3 **Prices** FF
Evening meal by request **Credit Cards** no **Children** yes
Closed never **Languages** English

Lavardens, N of Auch

Mascara

Deep in the country, a former storehouse is now a comfortable, two-storey cottage. Roger Hugon is artistic. Monique, a fine cook, organises gastronomic weekends in winter. Rustic and elegant furniture mix in the galleried sitting-room. Value for money.

Directions 22 km N of Auch. Take N 124, D 930. Continue on D 103 through Lavardens; house signposted 3 km beyond village.

❖ 32360 Lavardens **Tel** 62 64 52 17 **Rooms** 4 **Prices** FFF
Evening meal by request **Credit Cards** no **Children** yes **Closed** Jan
Languages English, German, Italian

Meyssac, SE of Brive

Manoir de Bellerade

Antiques preserve the 19thC ambience in this former home of a French colonial administrator. Jeanne Foussac-Lassalle's garden is immaculate, the bedrooms comfortable. Brunch, tea, simple or complex evening meals are available. Large park. Worth the price.
Directions 23 km SE of Brive. Take D 38; signposted between Collonges-la-Rouge and Meyssac. Up private driveway.

❖ 19500 Meyssac **Tel** 55 25 41 42 **Fax** 55 84 07 51 **Rooms** 3
Prices FF **Evening meal** by request **Credit Cards** no **Children** yes
Closed never **Languages** English, Spanish

Miélan, SW of Auch

La Tannerie

Carol and Barry Bryson are a British couple who have converted a handsome 19thC house in a village in the Pyrenean foothills. Furnishings include antiques and particularly comfortable beds. Carol cooks French dishes, serves local Madiran wines. Garden.
Directions 20 km SW of Auch. Take N 21 to Miélan. First street at entrance to village.

❖ chemin de la Fontaine, 32170 Miélan **Tel** 62 67 62 62 **Rooms** 3
Prices FF **Evening meal** by request **Credit Cards** V **Children** yes
Closed never **Languages** English

Montpitol, NE of Toulouse

Stoupignan

There is a restaurant two minutes' walk away, but don't ignore Claudette Fieux's authentic, if filling, local dishes such as *cassoulet*, *foie gras* and *poule au pot*. Her pretty early 17thC villa is in a wooded park with a sunny terrace for breakfast.
Directions 20 km NE of Toulouse. Take N 88 to Montastruc-la-Conseillère. Right on D 30. Stoupignan signposted after 4.5 km.

❖ 31380 Montpitol **Tel** 61 84 22 02 **Rooms** 4 **Prices** FFF
Evening meal by request **Credit Cards** no **Children** yes
Closed never **Languages** French only

St-André-du-Bois, NE of Langon

Château Malromé

One for art lovers and wine buffs. The Bordeaux vineyards surround this 14thC château where the painter, Toulouse-Lautrec, had a studio. He died here in 1901. The bedrooms are big and bare. Owner Jacques Foures makes and sells wine.
Directions 7 km NE of Langon. Take N 113, D 672 through Le Pian. Château signposted on left.

❖ 33490 St-André-du-Bois **Tel** 56 76 44 92 **Fax** 56 76 46 18 **Rooms** 7 **Prices** FFF **Evening meal** no **Credit Cards** V **Children** yes
Closed never **Languages** English

Moulin de la Garrigue

In a popular tourist region this is a pleasant setting: an old stone mill on a stream with half-timbered watch towers. Bedrooms, in a separate annexe, are well-decorated and have telephones. Large swimming-pool. The Vallée family treat this as a business.

Directions 10 km NW of Souillac. Take D 15, then D 62 towards Salignac. Signposted at Borrèze.

❖ Borrèze, 24590 Salignac **Tel** 53 28 84 88 **Rooms** 5 **Prices** FF **Evening meal** no **Credit Cards** no **Children** yes **Closed** never **Languages** French only

Tour St-Laurent

Set in a medieval village, Monique de la Borderie's carefully restored, circular 15thC tower provides a special experience. Local goose and wild mushrooms feature on her well-priced menus. Solid old furniture, modern bathrooms.

Directions 56 km S of Limoges. Take D 704 to St-Yrieix-la-Perche. Take D 18, D 6. Tower is opposite ruined castle.

❖ 19230 Ségur-le-Château **Tel** 55 73 54 17 **Rooms** 3 **Prices** FF **Evening meal** by request **Credit Cards** no **Children** yes **Closed** mid-Oct to mid-April **Languages** English

Domaine de Coutinard

Set in a large park in the outskirts of Turenne, Madame Jacques Continsouzas' handsome mansion has ivy-covered walls and a mansard roof. A grand staircase leads to the elegant bedrooms. A useful alternative to the Maison des Chanoines in town (page 130).

Directions 16 km SE of Brive. Take D 38, then D 8 to Turenne. Signposted.

❖ Coutinard, 19500 Turenne **Tel** 55 85 91 88 **Rooms** 3 **Prices** FF **Evening meal** by request **Credit Cards** no **Children** yes **Closed** never **Languages** English

Manoir La Barrière

In well-kept gardens, this 700-year-old, ochre stone manor house has been lovingly restored. The bedrooms have the privacy of their own entrances and guests can fish in the stream that runs through the grounds. Often booked by families for long holidays.

Directions 5 km E of Gourdon on D 673. On edge of village by the pond. Signposted.

❖ Le Vigan, 46300 Gourdon **Tel** 65 41 40 73 **Rooms** 5 **Prices** FFF **Evening meal** by request **Credit Cards** no **Children** yes **Closed** Oct to April **Languages** English, Spanish

---

Asprières, SE of Figeac

Le Mas de Clamouze

Visitors remark on the excellent value offered by Serge and Christine Maurel. The modern bedrooms are in a converted separate building with a sitting-room which doubles as a dining-room for evening meals. Swimming-pool, tennis-court.

Directions 16 km SE of Figeac. Take N 140 to Capdenac-Gare, then D 994 for Asprières; right on D 40. Sign on edge of village.

❖ 12700 Asprières **Tel** 65 63 89 89 **Rooms** 6 **Prices** FF
Evening meal by request **Credit Cards** no **Children** yes **Closed** Oct to April **Languages** English, German, Italian

---

Bellevue-la-Montagne, NW of Le Puy-en-Velay

Les Peupliers

This is a typical farm in the heart of France where bed-and-breakfast is secondary to working the land. Françoise Filère does not stint on portions at dinner. Useful for overnight stay or Chaise-Dieu musical festival (10 km), but bedrooms are plain.

Directions 28 km NW of Le Puy-en-Velay. N 102, D 906 for Thiers. La Monge is 2 km past Bellevue-la-Montagne. Follow signs.

❖ 43350 La Monge, Bellevue-la-Montagne **Tel** 71 00 60 54
Rooms 3 **Prices** FF **Evening meal** by request **Credit Cards** no
Children yes **Closed** never **Languages** French only

Castanet, NW of Albi

Naussens

In Madame Malbreil's modernised, old stone house, bedrooms have a separate entrance. Madame's evening meals might be: *charcuterie* with salad, then chicken, rabbit or duck, next local cheese, and finally a home-made gâteau. Awards for her garden.

Directions 12 km NW of Albi. Take D 600, then D 31 to Castanet on left. Naussens signposted.

❖ 81150 Castanet **Tel** 63 55 22 56 **Rooms** 2 **Prices** FF
Evening meal by request **Credit Cards** no **Children** yes
Closed never **Languages** some German

Chomelix, N of Le Puy-en-Velay

Miollet

Georges Marin and his wife are very house-proud, with slippers provided to climb the highly polished wooden staircase to bedrooms. Very clean though rather formal. Chaise-Dieu music festival (27 km).

Directions 35 km N of Le Puy-en-Velay. Take N 120, D 906 for Thiers. From Bellevue take D 1 to Miollet. House is 1 km beyond Chomelix on right.

❖ à Miollet par Chomelix, 43500 Craponne **Tel** 71 03 60 39
Rooms 4 **Prices** FF **Evening meal** by request **Credit Cards** no
Children yes **Closed** never **Languages** some English, Spanish

Quiers

High up in the Causses, above the Tarn River, with wonderful mountain views, the carefully restored stone farmhouse is a place to relax. Jean and Véronique Lombard-Pratmarty prepare unusually inventive and well-priced evening meals.
Directions 8 km N of Millau. Take N 9 through Aguessac; after 500 m turn right to Compeyre on D 547. Signposted in village.

❖ 12520 Compeyre **Tel** 65 59 85 10 **Rooms** 6 **Prices** FF
Evening meal by request **Credit Cards** no **Children** yes **Closed** Dec to March **Languages** French only

Paulagnac

Eliane and François Champel's attractive, modernised stone house is in the Livradois-Forez national park. Trees and hedges ensure further seclusion and shade in the flower-filled garden. Bedrooms have their own separate entrance.
Directions 4 km NE of Craponne-sur-Arzon. Take D 498; after 3 km follow signs on left. First house in Paulagnac.

❖ 43500 Craponne-sur-Arzon **Tel** 71 03 26 37 **Fax** 71 03 65 01
Rooms 3 **Prices** FFF **Evening meal** no **Credit Cards** no
Children yes **Closed** Oct to Easter **Languages** English

Vilherols

In a rugged part of Aveyron, Catherine Laurens' remote home of local pinkish-brown basalt has been well-restored. The surprisingly comfortable bedrooms have telephone, television, solid old furniture and separate entrances. Well-priced. Restaurants 3 km.
Directions 30 km N of Entraygues-sur-Truyère. Take D 904; 4 km after Lacroix-Barrez, follow signs on right.

❖ 12600 Lacroix-Barrez **Tel** 65 66 08 24 **Fax** 65 66 19 98 **Rooms** 3
Prices FF **Evening meal** no **Credit Cards** no **Children** yes
Closed never **Languages** English

Le Courtiau

An unpretentious country cottage with green shutters, set in a pretty garden in farmland. Madame Iannotti is very proud of her new interior-sprung mattresses. One bedroom in the main house has extra beds for children. Useful overnight stop.
Directions 35 km S of Moulins. N 9 to St Pourçain. Turn W on D 46. Louchy-Montfand on left. House signposted from village.

❖ 03500 Louchy-Montfand **Tel** 70 45 91 03 **Rooms** 3 **Prices** FF
Evening meal no **Credit Cards** no **Children** yes **Closed** Nov to mid-March **Languages** Italian

Mezens, NE of Toulouse

Le Cambou

Henri and Régine Saulle-Bultau teach weaving and sculpting. In the 200-year-old house with original stone floors, the bedrooms are plain with cheap, modern furniture. Adequate, nothing more.
Directions 35 km NE of Toulouse. Take N 88; at St Sulpice-la-Pointe, take first left on D 28; drive through Mezens. House is second road on right past church, second house on right.

❖ 81800 Mezens, St-Sulpice-la-Pointe **Tel** 63 41 82 66 **Rooms** 3
Prices FF **Evening meal** by request **Credit Cards** no **Children** yes
Closed mid-Dec to mid-Jan **Languages** English, Dutch

Rodelle, N of Rodez

Domaine de la Goudalie

A large, sheltered swimming-pool stands in the shadow of the Mouyssets' massive 19thC stone house on the Causse de Lanhac. The large bedrooms are useful for families but with seven *gîtes* also on site, this can feel like a holiday camp.
Directions 26 km N of Rodez. Take D 988, D 904, then D 68 for Rodelle. Signs on right after Bezonnes.

❖ 12340 Rodelle **Tel** 65 46 90 00 **Fax** 65 43 06 66 **Rooms** 4
Prices FF **Evening meal** no **Credit Cards** no **Children** yes
Closed Nov to March **Languages** French only

St-Front, SE of Le Puy

Les Bastides du Mezenc

Prizes should be given for finding this remote mountain village. Rooms in the stone farmhouse are rustic but popular with alpine and downhill skiers. Paul Coffy is a professional sled-dog driver; Nadège prepares generous meals including Swiss-style *raclette*.
Directions 25 km SE of Le Puy. D 15 to les Pandraux; right on D 36 via Laussonne to D 500; left for Fay. Signs in St-Front.

❖ 43550 St-Front **Tel** 71 59 51 57 **Rooms** 4 **Prices** FF
Evening meal by request **Credit Cards** no **Children** yes
Closed never **Languages** English, Spanish

St-Privat-du-Dragon, SE of Brioude

Chambord

Marie-Paule and Alain Bisson are still renovating this lovely old stone house, in the hills near the Allier River. Although they are getting used to the concept of bed-and-breakfast, there is still a lack of warmth and comfort. Some personal touches needed.
Directions SE of Brioude. Take N 102 for Le Puy. After 16 km right at la Chomette on D 41. Signs in St-Privat.

❖ 43380 St-Privat-du-Dragon **Tel** 71 76 64 32 **Rooms** 5
Prices FF **Evening meal** by request **Credit Cards** no **Children** yes
Closed Oct to May **Languages** English

Ste-Geneviève, NE of Entraygues-sur-Truyère

Le Boukarou

One of a kind, thanks to the many souvenirs of the years the Mallers spent in Africa. Beyond the picture windows is the *boukarou,* a thatched African hut. Comfortable bedrooms.
Directions 30 km NE of Entraygues-sur-Truyère. Take D 904 to Mur-de-Barrez; then D 900, D 166, D 98, D 537 to Ste-Geneviève-sur-Argence. On right just beyond village.

❖ 12420 St-Geneviève-sur-Argence **Tel** 65 66 41 32 **Rooms** 2
Prices FFF **Evening meal** no **Credit Cards** no **Children** yes
Closed never **Languages** French only

Verneix, NE of Montluçon

Château de Fragne

This beautifully proportioned, 18thC château has seen better days. The grounds are rather overgrown, some rooms are musty. The Comtesse de Montaignac seems delighted to have some company. Bedrooms are adequate, evening meals overpriced.
Directions 12 km NE of Montluçon. Take D 94, after crossing D 39, turn left up driveway.

❖ 03190 Verneix **Tel** 70 07 88 10 **Fax** 70 07 83 73 **Rooms** 5
Prices FFFF **Evening meal** by request **Credit Cards** AE V
Children yes **Closed** Nov to April **Languages** English, Spanish

Verneuil-en-Bourbonnais, S of Moulins

Demeure de Chaumejean

An attractive house with imposing entrance, walled garden and lofty rooms. Most guests come here to take week-long pottery courses with Christian Sarrazin. High-quality furniture and linens but rather too business-like, lacking the personal touch.
Directions 30 km S of Moulins. N9 for St Pourçain. Just before St Pourçain, right on D 18. Verneuil on left; house signposted.

❖ 03500 Verneuil-en-Bourbonnais **Tel** 70 45 53 92 **Rooms** 5
Prices FF **Evening meal** no **Credit Cards** no **Children** yes
Closed Jan **Languages** English, some Spanish

Vieille-Brioude, S of Brioude

La Coustade

This is not romantic. The plain, modern house, with its annexe, is purpose-built so bedrooms are large enough for a table and chair. Anne-Marie and Gérard Chantel are relatively new to the business but very friendly. Good reports on evening meals.
Directions 4 km S of Brioude. Take N 102 for Le Puy. Before Vieille-Brioude turn left on Chemin du Stade; follow signs.

❖ Chemin du Stade, 43100 Vieille-Brioude **Tel** 71 50 25 21
Rooms 5 **Prices** FF **Evening meal** by request **Credit Cards** no
Children yes **Closed** Nov to Mar **Languages** French only

Barjac, NW of Pont-St-Esprit
Rue Basse

Near the famous gorges of the Ardèche river, Jean-Claude Ciaramella's restored 18thC village house is in the middle of a well-kept, walled garden. Inside, huge rooms boast vaulted ceilings, solid, old furniture. Swimming-pool. Restaurants nearby.
Directions 32 km NW of Pont-St-Esprit. Take N 86, D 901 to Barjac. Signposted in rue Basse.

❖ rue Basse, 30430 Barjac **Tel** 66 24 59 63 **Rooms** 3 **Prices** FF **Evening meal** no **Credit Cards** no **Children** yes **Closed** never **Languages** French only

---

Cases-de-Pène, NW of Perpignan
Domaine Habana

A modern estate in the hills above Perpignan where Michel Lescadieu's own wines accompany excellent evening meals, with fish a feature. Bedrooms have television, telephone and pretty, tiled bathrooms. Beaches nearby, fine swimming-pool on site.
Directions 15 km NW of Perpignan. Take D 117 to Cases-de-Pène. Follow signs to house.

❖ 66600 Cases-de-Pène **Tel** 68 38 91 70 **Fax** 68 38 92 64 **Rooms** 6 **Prices** FFF **Evening meal** by request **Credit Cards** V **Children** yes **Closed** never **Languages** English, Spanish

---

Castelnou, SW of Perpignan
Domaine de Querubi

Surrounded by olive trees, the ochre farmhouse sits on a huge estate in the foothills of the Pyrenees. Modern bedrooms have television, telephone. Françoise Nabet's cooking, especially her desserts, win praise. Swimming-pool, mountain bikes, horse riding.
Directions 21 km SW of Perpignan. Take D 612a to Thuir, then D 48 through Castelnou. House 3 km beyond castle.

❖ 66300 Castelnou **Tel** 68 53 19 08 **Fax** 68 53 18 96 **Rooms** 5 **Prices** FFF **Evening meal** by request **Credit Cards** V **Children** yes **Closed** never **Languages** Spanish

---

Fayence
Ferme des Moulières

Young families feel at ease in this modern house set in vineyards. The Moranges have children and dogs, so the ambience is chaotic yet appealing. Only one bedroom has a private bath. He is French, keeps bees. She is Romanian, paints, teaches yoga.
Directions 8 km S of Fayence. Take D 563, D 4. Follow signs in St-Paul-en-Forêt. House on D 55.

❖ St-Paul-en-Forêt, 83440 Fayence **Tel** 94 84 17 07 **Rooms** 5 **Prices** FF **Evening meal** by request **Credit Cards** no **Children** yes **Closed** mid-Oct to mid-March **Languages** English, German, Italian, Romanian

---

Lacoste, SW of Apt

Domaine Layaude-Basse

On the edge of the village, Olivier and Lydia Mazel's popular bed-and-breakfast is in a garden with swings, mature trees and a small but attractive swimming-pool. The evening meal is fair value. There are winter weekend courses for four-wheel driving.
Directions 16 km SW of Apt. Take N 100 for Avignon. Turn left on D 36, right on D 108. Follow signs in village.

❖ 84710 Lacoste **Tel** 90 75 90 06 **Fax** 90 75 99 03 **Rooms** 5 **Prices** FFF **Evening meal** by request **Credit Cards** no **Children** yes **Closed** never **Languages** French only

---

Oppède, E of Avignon

La Cerisaie

The name gives a clue: cherry orchards surround Pierre Marchand's renovated Provençal farmhouse. Colette's cooking is praised. One bedroom is air-conditioned. Bicycles and swimming-pool available for guests. Short season.
Directions 35 km E of Avignon. Take N 7, D 22. Turn right on D 178 to village. Follow signs.

❖ route d'Apt, 84580 Oppède **Tel** 90 76 91 34 **Rooms** 5 **Prices** FF **Evening meal** by request **Credit Cards** no **Children** yes **Closed** mid-May to mid-June; Oct to mid-March **Languages** French only

---

Orange

Domaine la Violette

Don't be deceived by the surrounding wheatfields; a railway line runs nearby. Otherwise, this converted farmhouse is peaceful, despite the Alsatian dogs. Prices are somewhat high for the bedrooms; the evening meal is better value. Swimming-pool.
Directions on northern edge of city. Take N7; turn right after Arc de Triomphe into avenue Jean-Moulin. Poorly signposted.

❖ chemin de Lauriol, 84100 Orange **Tel** 90 51 57 09 **Fax** 90 34 86 15 **Rooms** 5 **Prices** FFF **Evening meal** by request **Credit Cards** no **Children** yes **Closed** never **Languages** English

---

Paradou, NE of Arles

Le Mazet des Alpilles

Surrounded by evergreens, the suburban modern house is set back from the road; it won a prize for its flower garden in 1992. The furnishings are rather old-fashioned and redecoration is urgently needed. Micheline Letailleur is shy but helpful. A useful base.
Directions 15 km NE of Arles. Take D 17 towards Fontvieille, then D 82 for Paradou. Bear right on D 78. House well-signed.

❖ Le Bas Paradou, route de Brunelly, 13125 Paradou **Tel** 90 54 45 89 **Rooms** 3 **Prices** FF **Evening meal** no **Credit Cards** no **Children** yes **Closed** never **Languages** French only

---

Plaissan, W of Montpellier

9 rue des Prunus

In a small village in the parched countryside, Michel and Danièle Colin's turn-of-the-century wine grower's house recalls the 1930s with its beds, chairs and murals. Guests have the use of a kitchen for light meals and picnics. Restaurant one minute away.
Directions 43 km W of Montpellier. Take N 109 to Gignac. Left on D 32 to Canet crossroads; left again on D 2 to Plaissan.

❖ 9 rue des Prunus, 34230 Plaissan **Tel** 67 96 81 16 **Rooms** 4
Prices FF **Evening meal** no **Credit Cards** no **Children** yes
Closed never **Languages** French only

Pomérols, SE of Pézenas

Domaine Fon de Rey

Although this ivy-covered, 17thC house is inland among the vineyards, the sea is visible from the garden. Tall pines surround the outdoor swimming-pool. Alain Poisson has a stained glass workshop; his wife Céline is a professional cook.
Directions 10 km SE of Pézenas. A 9 to Agde exit. Head for St-Thibéry; D 18 to Pomérols. House 1 km N of Pomérols on D 161.

❖ Route de Pézenas, 34810 Pomérols **Tel and Fax** 67 77 08 56
Rooms 6 **Prices** FF **Evening meal** by request **Credit Cards** no
Children yes **Closed** never **Languages** English, Spanish

Revens-Trèves, E of Millau

L'Ermitage St-Pierre

The canyon of the Dourbie River is a scenic highlight in the Causses. The stone priory, with 1,000 years of history, has been made habitable by Madeleine Macq. One bedroom has a small kitchen; two have four-poster beds. A memorable experience.
Directions 21 km E of Millau. Take D 991. Signposted after 21 km; by the road.

❖ 30750 Revens-Trèves **Tel** 65 62 27 99 **Rooms** 5 **Prices** FF
Evening meal by request, off-season **Credit Cards** no **Children** yes
Closed never **Languages** French only

Ribaute-les-Tavernes, S of Alès

Château de Ribaute

In the pretty Gardon d'Anduze valley, the ancestral home of the Comte and Comtesse Chamski-Mandajors dates back to the 13thC though most is 18thC. Elegant rooms have antiques. An expensive experience, breakfast is extra. Swimming-pool.
Directions 12 km S of Alès. Take N 110 to les Tavernes. Right on D 106 to Ribaute-les-Tavernes. Signposted.

❖ 30720 Ribaute-les-Tavernes **Tel** 66 83 01 66 **Fax** 66 83 86 93
Rooms 5 **Prices** FFFF **Evening meal** by request **Credit Cards** MC V
Children yes **Closed** never **Languages** English

St-André-de-Buèges, NW of Montpellier

Bombequiols

On a small golf course, this carefully restored *bastide* (fortified farmhouse) offers luxury in a beautiful mountain setting. Worth the expense, especially since Anne-Marie Bouec's meals, using local produce and wines, are a bargain. Swimming-pool.
Directions 40 km NW of Montpellier. D 986 to St-Bauzille-de-Putois; left on D 108; follow signs to 'Golf de Bombequiols'.

❖ 34190 St-André-de-Buèges **Tel** 67 73 72 67 **Fax** 67 73 33 24
Rooms 6 **Prices** FFFF **Evening meal** by request **Credit Cards** no
Children yes **Closed** never; book ahead **Languages** French only

---

St-Nazaire-des-Gardies, NW of Nîmes

Mas de la Fauguière

Surrounded by fields and woods, what was once a silk farm has been restored by British owner Edna Price. Bedrooms are tastefully decorated, comfortable. Most guests relax here, lazing by the swimming-pool. Restaurants, *ferme auberge* nearby.
Directions 44 km NW of Nîmes. D 999 to Quissac; right on D 35; right on D 182 before St-Jean; left after 1.5 km to La Fauguière.

❖ St-Nazaire-des-Gardies, 30610 Sauve **Tel** 66 77 38 67 **Fax** 66 77
11 64 **Rooms** 2 **Prices** FFF **Evening meal** no **Credit Cards** no
Children yes **Closed** never **Languages** English, German

Vaison-la-Romaine, NE of Orange

Les Cigales

The Hortes are retired doctors who love opera and even sing for guests. Their bungalow, on a countrified housing estate on the edge of the famous town, is a clean, serviceable alternative if nearby recommendations are full. Bedrooms have separate entrances.
Directions 35 km NE of Orange. Take N 7, D 977. On edge of Vaison-la-Romaine.

❖ chemin des Abeilles, 84110 Vaison-la-Romaine **Tel** 90 36 02 25
Rooms 5 **Prices** FF **Evening meal** no **Credit Cards** no **Children** no
Closed Oct to March **Languages** English, German

Villetelle, SW of Nîmes

Les Bougainvilliers

On the edge of the village, Simone and Daniel Barlaguet's modern, Provençal-style bungalow is some 20 km from the sea. Active guests use the tennis-court, swimming-pool, Jacuzzi. Bedrooms, on the ground floor, have terraces, central heating. No pets.
Directions 24 km SW of Nîmes. N 113 to Lunel; right on D 34; fork right on D 110 E to village. Hard to find; ask for directions.

❖ 343 chemin des Combes Noires, 34400 Villetelle **Tel** 67 71 26 16
Fax 66 53 30 77 **Rooms** 6 **Prices** FF **Evening meal** by request
Credit Cards no **Children** yes **Closed** never; telephone in advance
Languages English

Li Fundali

High on Cap Corse, Corsica's northern finger, Alain Gabelle has four bedrooms in an attractive stone house next to his home and a fortified tower. Guests have use of a sitting-room with television. Evening meals are a bargain. The coast is 8 km east or west.
Directions 36 km N of Bastia. Take D 80 to Sta-Severa. Left on D 180 to Luri. Signposted.

❖ 20228 Luri **Tel** 95 35 06 15 **Rooms** 4 **Prices** FF **Evening meal** by request **Credit Cards** no **Children** yes **Closed** never
Languages French only

Auberge du Barrage

A popular spot for outings, the simple *ferme auberge* is up a twisting road, high in the hills above l'Ile-Rousse. By a lake on the dammed Regino river, Mme Francisci has five plain bedrooms above her restaurant. Down-to-earth; no pets.
Directions 8 km SE of l'Ile-Rousse. Take D 63 via Monticello to Regino. Small, winding road. Well-signposted.

❖ Regino, 20281 Speloncato **Tel** 95 61 50 31 **Rooms** 5 **Prices** FF **Evening meal** in *auberge* **Credit Cards** no **Children** yes **Closed** Oct to March **Languages** French only

---

Villa Les Prairies

In the Castagniccia region, known for its chestnut trees, rugged landscape and cooler climate, Mme Marie Fontana has just one spare bedroom in her home, so this is the traditional bed-and-breakfast where you join in with your host. Quite a drive.
Directions 52 km S of Bastia. Take N 193, N 198 to Folelli. Right on D 506; left on D 236, D 36. Signs in Scata.

❖ 20264 Scata **Tel** 95 36 95 90 **Rooms** 1 **Prices** FF **Evening meal** by request **Credit Cards** no **Children** yes **Closed** never; telephone in winter **Languages** French only

---

U Celavu

No more than a useful place for an overnight stay since this is plain, rustic and somewhat noisy, near the main road from Ajaccio to the north and east of the island. Bedrooms are part of François Orsoni's *ferme auberge* which is touristy.
Directions 22 km NE of Ajaccio. Take N 193 to Suaricchio. On main road.

❖ 20133 Suaricchio **Tel** 95 52 80 64 **Rooms** 4 **Prices** FF **Evening meal** in *auberge* **Credit Cards** no **Children** yes **Closed** never; telephone in winter **Languages** French only

Index

Index

Index

Index

Index

Index

Index

Index

Index